YES, YOU CAN HOMESCHOOL!

THE TERRIFIED PARENT'S COMPANION TO HOMESCHOOL SUCCESS

ERIN A. BARRY

Edited by
BRETT BARRY

YES, YOU CAN HOMESCHOOL!
by Erin A. Barry

Published by
Inseparable Lives, LLC in association with
The Home Educated Mind
www.inseparablelives.com / www.them.company

ISBN: 978-1948339278

Copyright © 2018 Erin A. Barry

For permissions contact:
info@inseparablelives.com

Printed in the United States of America 2018

First Edition

YES, YOU CAN HOMESCHOOL!

The Terrified Parent's Companion To Homeschool Success

By Erin A. Barry

Dedicated to my parents, Mano and Sheila Constantinidis — my first teachers and mentors

ACKNOWLEDGMENTS

This book would not be a reality without the tremendous help and support of many wonderful and gifted friends and family.

First, I cannot adequately express my gratitude to my husband, Brett Barry, who consistently and tenderly believed in me when I doubted myself to be the lead learner throughout our homeschooling journey. Then, specifically with this book, from editing and helping nuance the ideas, to strengthening and crafting my writing voice, to designing the cover and support materials, his hand is all through it. Beyond that, creating our websites, writing the copy and organizing, designing and leading all the marketing strategies that go into a project like this, he has believed in and supported me in every way possible. Brett, I was smitten with you 30 years ago, and today I can't imagine my life without you—we are, inseparable.

Secondly, I am so grateful to those that read my first draft attempt. Amiee Bowersox, for your wise and intuitive input, and my SOAP Bible Study friends, Rae Holbrook, Angie Joy, Paula Sachsenmeier and Liz VanBrunt, for your insightful feedback and editing eyes, but most of all for our years of faithful friendship that reach so far beyond the scope of this project.

Thirdly, I want to thank my book launch team under the leadership of Kaytee Cobb. Your support, encouragement, input and companionship throughout this project have been life-giving.

I can't begin to name the many others of my family and friends who have supported me and prayed with me throughout this endeavor. Please know it has meant the world to me.

To our three children, Lauren, Brooks and Pierz, who were my practice for this writing, I treasure our homeschooling years and the privilege of growing and learning together. I couldn't be more proud of who you have become.

Finally, I cannot sufficiently convey my gratefulness to The Lord. God, Your kindness and steadfast, long-suffering love is overwhelming, and I acknowledge that only through You is this journey and work possible. Thank You.

CONTENTS

SECTION 4 – Reflections at the End of the Journey

APPENDIX

PREFACE

Before we begin, I want to share a few personal views so you will have a better understanding of where I am coming from as we look at the various topics I'll be covering.

I am a Christian with a Biblical worldview.

It's important that my readers understand up front that I am processing and communicating through a Biblical worldview.

First, a worldview is the core beliefs or lens through which we view the world—what we believe about God, the origin of humanity, our purpose for existing, right and wrong, and so on. We all have a set of core beliefs, and these beliefs affect what we value most in life and, ultimately, how we behave (or aspire to). So when I use the term "Biblical worldview," this means that I believe the Bible contains the answers to life's most important questions, and that it contains absolute truth as found in the person of Jesus Christ. It also means that I believe it reveals God's objective authority, intent and provision regarding the humanity He created. Our family therefore views Scripture as the God-given standard to direct our lives and priorities; that it is something we therefore submit to and, as challenging as it can be at times, honor in its entirety.

I realize you may hold a different worldview. Regardless, I am confident there are many principles in this book that you will find helpful should you choose to read on.

Pray and ask the Lord how you should educate your family, then do what He says.

Start reading in pretty much any chapter and you will quickly conclude that I am a homeschool advocate. Brett (my husband) and I believe in it wholeheartedly. In fact, we value it to such a degree that our family has sacrificed to do it. However, as much as I will identify and proclaim the benefits and wisdom of homeschooling throughout the following pages, and as much as I believe it is God's intent for parents to be engaged with their children at the level homeschooling naturally affords, I do not believe it is wrong to educate our children through other avenues.

I say this because I sometimes encounter parents who feel pressured by others or guilty because they want to homeschool but cannot. So, while I'm going to champion home education, please know I recognize and support the reality of exceptions.

As stated, the key is, and this is true for anyone seeking a relationship with God, are we asking God (praying) what His will is for our family, and then, by His strength, doing what He says?

The Bible says a lot about the parent's responsibility to intentionally train our children in the Lord, so we definitely need to be deliberate and diligent when it comes to raising them in His ways. But it does not specify that in order to do so we have to homeschool. Rather, it instructs us to "train up a child in the way he should go" Proverbs 22:6 and to "bring them up in the training and admonition of the Lord" Ephesians 6:4. In Deuteronomy

11:19-21, regarding His commands, He proclaims, "You shall teach them to your children, speaking of them when you sit in your house, when you walk by the way, when you lie down, and when you rise up. And you shall write them on the doorposts of your house and on your gates, that your days and the days of your children may be multiplied..."

If the Lord directs you to other avenues of education, then by all means, do it. But I encourage you to do so through prayer, being fully aware of the environment your children will be in, especially in public school (see Appendix), and to go forward with a plan for strategically addressing that influence.

It is Jesus who saves, not homeschooling.

I wish I could promise you that if you homeschool your children they will be Christians who faithfully listen to God and obey Him! But it doesn't work that way. Statistically, homeschooled children are more likely to maintain their parent's beliefs and values than children raised in public school, but there are no guarantees. They can still choose to reject them. Children eventually have to develop their own relationship with God through Jesus. As our Pastor often says, "God has no grandchildren." Each person has to work out their own salvation in Jesus. The advantage of homeschooling in this regard is that you can be sure the gospel is clearly taught and a relationship with Jesus modeled on a consistent basis.

You are not a better parent if you homeschool.

You are not a better parent if you homeschool. Similarly, neither is a person a better parent if they have home births or use cloth diapers or don't watch TV! What makes us good parents is that we love and nurture our children in the admonition of the Lord to the best of our ability. Parenting is hard work! All of us know our weaknesses only too well. We don't need to put more guilt and pressure on each other. Now, if you're not feeding your children, then yes, that would be considered bad parenting. But we need to be careful about including preferences or practices as indicators of being good parents or not. And while we are at it... neither are we a better parent if we have more children! The number of children you have is not a measure of your goodness, but of God's goodness. He says children are a blessing. So if you have a bunch of kids—thank the Lord! You are blessed!

Overall, we need to be careful we're not making claims that God did not make, thereby putting unnecessary guilt and pressure on others or ourselves.

Not everyone can homeschool.

Finally, there are many legitimate reasons that not everyone can homeschool. Maybe a person is a single parent and is the only source of income for their family. Maybe they're caring for aging parents. Or perhaps a parent feels called to be part of a local school or private school community. Or, what if a husband and wife are not in agreement with homeschooling their children? Ultimately, a couple who wrestles through an issue and comes to agreement in a united front will do more for the wellbeing of the child than homeschooling can in an environment of discord. There are more resources than ever to help people in all kinds of circumstances all over the world to be able to homeschool, which is really exciting. But it may not be your path, or simply not your season right now.

For those contemplating homeschooling:

While there is encouragement and insights in the following pages for parents at any stage of their homeschool journey, my purpose in writing this book is to help those who are curious or considering homeschooling, but for various reasons are hesitant or downright *terrified*! If that's you, you're in the right place. Whatever your fears or concerns, this book is for you! It was written to help parents understand that homeschooling provides a valid, tested and excellent education—one that parents can effectively facilitate, and to bring perspective to the amazing role and opportunity we have in helping mentor our children toward the whole persons God intends for them to become.

So if you feel even the slightest tug to homeschool, I want to encourage you and help you to pursue it! We'll work on the fear factor, but just know that if you ask me, I'm going to say, "Yes, you can homeschool!"

INTRODUCTION

Have you ever considered homeschooling your children but then been overcome with thoughts of fear and inadequacy? "Will my children be weird?" "What about socialization?" "Am I smart enough or competent enough to be their teacher?" "What if I ruin them or their future?"

Or, maybe you've worried that home educating will cause them to miss out on important academic or collective experiences. "Will they have any friends? Any *normal* friends?" "What about prom?" "What about sports?" "Will they get into college?" And the list goes on.

Most parents ask many questions like these when considering the idea of educating their children at home. I know I sure did. Every one of those questions and more plagued my mind as we jumped in...plus, it was nearly 20 years ago when I first began wrestling my many concerns. Homeschooling wasn't popular and the available helps and success stories were pretty much nil.

Our introduction to homeschooling was much like the final scene of the movie, *Finding Nemo*: The aquarium fish have planned and plotted throughout the entire story to escape the confinement of the dentist's tank. Finally, they are victorious! They clog up the filter, get themselves transferred into water-filled, plastic bags and end up hopping out the window, crossing the busy highway and jumping into the ocean!

Still in their plastic bags and now bobbing on the surface of the vast ocean waters they cheer at their glorious success and the sheer genius of their plan. There's a moment of silence. And, as the reality of their new confinement obstacle begins to sink in, the blowfish sums up the perplexity of their situation: "Now What?"

Yep. That was the atmosphere in the late 1990's. We had gotten into the ocean so to speak, but we had no idea how to go forward from there. As mentioned, at that point in the United States there were only a handful of curricula and resources, and an equally scarce number of people who had homeschooled successfully to help others navigate. Homeschooling itself had only recently been legalized in certain states.

Today, however, it's a different story. Homeschooling is a growing choice for education all over the world and is taking place on every continent. There is an abundance of curricula, seemingly endless resources and just as many success stories to glean from. I am one. I have homeschooled all three of our children from kindergarten through high school, plus assisted and mentored many other students and parents over the years. To our humble delight, our oldest will graduate from college in a few months, our second is a college junior and our youngest a college freshman; all are in honors programs and maintaining high GPA's.

If you had told me in 1997 that my future included successfully homeschooling all three of our children, I would have thought you were crazy! I would have told you all the reasons why there was *no way* I was capable of accomplishing such a task, and that I wasn't convinced I even wanted to.

But take heart, my friend. In the following pages I am going to address your fears, doubts and questions, and demonstrate why you are not only more capable of homeschooling than you think, but that you are the best possible choice to manage your child's education.

I am going to share my personal mistakes and imperfections, along with some of my victories, so you will be confident that, if I can homeschool successfully, anyone can!

I am going to share tips and lessons I have learned along the way so that you don't have to reinvent the wheel.

I am going to talk about the different types of learners, how all children are different, even in the same home (my children included), and give examples of how we coped.

I am going to explain how public education has changed and share facts you need to seriously consider when making the decision of what system (public, private, homeschool) is best for your family.

I am going to demonstrate that homeschooling is not a foreign concept but a trusted method of effective education, and that public education is actually a rather new concept.

I am going to share about God's faithfulness and how through His strength He not only covered our weaknesses, but led and empowered us to complete this journey.

Understanding the answers and perspectives of these foundational questions and common reservations will help you better articulate your vision for homeschooling, feel confident in embarking on the journey, and keep you committed and empowered when the pressures and challenges arise.

Again, homeschooling was our family's choice, but it may not be yours, and that is okay. As stated, my purpose in writing this book is to inform and thereby calm fear, and to encourage and empower those who think they may want to join this exciting, international and cutting-edge form of education. And, equally so, it is to help parents see the value of their intentional and direct involvement in their child's education.

Section 1

WHAT ABOUT SOCIALIZATION?

"The philosophy of the school room in one generation, will be the philosophy of government in the next."

Abraham Lincoln

WHAT ABOUT SOCIALIZATION?

The number one question I hear from those considering homeschooling is, "What about socialization?" Our family was no exception.

One day my neighbor who had recently moved in next door, whom I'll call Jennifer, said with great astonishment, "I saw your daughter the other day and...well...she looked normal!"

At first, I wasn't sure about the context of her statement. Why would she think otherwise? Then I remembered. We'd had a conversation a couple days earlier where she asked me if I knew of any college students who might be able to babysit her six year old daughter in the mornings from 7:00 AM. until she caught her bus for school. I had mentioned my 16 year old daughter, Laurén, as a candidate for the job because she was homeschooled and available at that time. (I am always trying to employ my children, as I believe strongly in the value of having work experience and learning to manage money!) I added, "Laurén is great with children, and since we live right next door, it would be convenient and easy."

Jennifer had hesitated, and I assumed it was because she

hadn't met Laurén. I solved the problem by promising to introduce them as soon as possible.

But that wasn't her concern! What I didn't realize was that the word "homeschool" produced visions of an awkward, socially maladjusted teenager dressed in dated clothing and hair style who we only let out to go to church on Sundays—with a chaperone! So, when Jennifer actually saw Laurén, she was shocked and taken aback that she wasn't a misfit. She was relieved that our daughter seemed like a typical teenager, one that might actually be able to interact with people and survive in the real world. Someone worth hiring.

In Jennifer's defense, we were the first homeschooling family she had ever met. Like many people, she had a preconceived notion of what homeschoolers were like. I had been in the homeschool world eleven years when this incident occurred, so I had resolved my fears of socialization. But if you are new to homeschooling, you too may have legitimate questions about socialization. If you do, Section 1 is for you.

Define Your Terms

The first rule of logic is to define your terms. This rule exists because it is very important to make sure that when you are discussing something with someone you both have the same understanding of what various terms mean. So, when this question of socialization comes up, I usually ask the person to explain what they mean by socialization. I have found that most people aren't quite sure what it really means, but they know it is important.

Dictionary.com defines socialization as "a continuing process whereby an individual acquires a personal identity and learns the norms, values, behavior, and social skills appropriate to his or her social position."[1]

After defining the word, in most cases the person realizes that when discussing socialization in the context of homeschooling they are usually talking about something other than what the term actually means. Instead, they have been referring to children not getting the social skills and experiences common and prized in the typical childhood or adolescent school years; experiences such as friends, prom, sports, college entrance, etc., which I will address in later chapters.

But professionals understand and use socialization according to its definition, which also closely resembles the definition of culture in The Essentials of Sociology, a text used for the first year college level course, Sociology 101:

 "Culture is the values, norms, and material goods characteristic of a given group...values, are abstract ideals. For example, monogamy—being faithful to a single marriage partner is a prominent value in most Western societies ...Norms are widely agreed upon principles or rules people are expected to observe, they represent the do's and don'ts of social life... Material goods refer to the physical objects that individuals in society create. These objects in turn influence how we live. They include the food we eat, the clothes we wear, the cars we drive to the houses we live in..."[2]

Language and the symbols a society reveres are included in the discussion about culture as well. When educators or psychologists express concern about homeschooled children not being "socialized" they are suggesting that the apprehension of the transmission of our culture to these students is not being accomplished. As stated, that is a very different question than most parents who are considering homeschooling are thinking of when they mention fear about socialization.

But both aspects, the passing of culture norms, values, symbols, and material goods etc., and the rite of passage, whether homeschooled children are getting the academic skills and social experiences usually associated with school, do matter. The remainder of Section 1 will deal with the former and Section 2 will address the latter.

In the discussion we will consider the dictionary definition, as it is important and worth discussing. But before we go too far into answering "What about socialization?" we need to clearly define it, and then answer such questions as, Whose job is it to socialize our children? What part does school play in socialization? And finally, What is or should be the purpose of education?

WHOSE JOB IS IT TO SOCIALIZE OUR CHILDREN

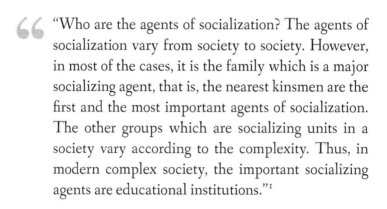

"Who are the agents of socialization? The agents of socialization vary from society to society. However, in most of the cases, it is the family which is a major socializing agent, that is, the nearest kinsmen are the first and the most important agents of socialization. The other groups which are socializing units in a society vary according to the complexity. Thus, in modern complex society, the important socializing agents are educational institutions."[1]

The socialization process in our culture typically begins at home, with parents being the predominant influence in a child's growth and care. As children grow, however, more and more people play a part in their development.

Once children reach school age their peers and educators become a major influence in their lives, often the prominent influence. We don't normally think of schools as a socializing agent, rather, we see them as academic institutions. This may be due to the tendency to compartmentalize different aspects of development. But it's important to understand how deeply inter-twined school and socialization actually are.

Additionally, it's easy to perceive socialization as being social. So when considering homeschooling it's natural to think that if our children aren't with the masses they will not learn to be social or make friends. Nearly all of us can picture the naïve, stereotypical image of a homeschooled person as alluded to in the introductory story.

To bring clarity to the distinction, however, I would like to address both elements of socialization: what it means to be social and how school is a socializing agent.

What It Means to Be Social

Most parents I speak with think of the first meaning, being social, when they hear the word socialization. With that they tend to associate the need for a large group to accomplish the goal of being social. But being in a larger group doesn't necessarily equate to better social experiences or stronger social skills. For some, particularly an introvert, the large group can be quite daunting and overwhelming to manage.

What most people desire when discussing being social is relationship, which is accomplished through meaningful connection with others and, interestingly, occurs more often within a smaller circle of people.

Consider the work done by "Robin Dunbar, a University of Oxford anthropologist and psychologist in his study, which he started in the 1980's. He developed the Machiavellian Intelligence Hypothesis, which made predictions of the size of social groups for animals based on the size of their frontal lobe. He then transitioned his findings and used his formula to make predictions about people. "For the last twenty-two years Dunbar has been 'unpacking and exploring' what that number actually means

—and whether our ever-expanding social networks have done anything to change it."[2]

To summarize Dunbar's findings, he noted we have between 100-200 causal friends, out of whom we have about 50 friends we'd invite to a dinner party, and then from that group about 15 people would fall into our support group and, finally, 5 people would be considered our closest friends, which interestingly often included family members. Scripture supports this theory when analyzing social circles based on Jesus. Scholars note Jesus had an outer circle of about 500 people, then 70, then his support group of twelve, and within the twelve, he was closer to three, James, John, and Peter. The Apostle John often is considered his best friend.

I bring this up because people often struggle with the thought of not being a part of a large school system. They reason that if they homeschool it will limit their children's opportunities for friends and relationships and, ultimately, their skills of being social. Honestly, being a very social person myself, I was initially concerned as well. But this is not the case, because the issue is not about numbers but developing an inner circle of deep relationships.

Today, there are so many options to make friends and have social gatherings. There are coops, classes, groups and organizations, all designed specifically for homeschoolers, along with regular community organizations and churches. Personally, we did not lack social interaction at all. And I was surprised to find, just as the research indicates, that the smaller groups often provided stronger, more manageable relational circles. Plus, as I will cover later, in large classrooms or school yards, the negative peer pressure can be an unwanted social pressure.

Homeschooled Student Socialization Research

There have been numerous studies conducted to assess the socialization skills of homeschooled children, i.e., their ability to socially interact with others. The findings are that this kind of socialization is not a problem for homeschoolers; to the contrary, they actually tend to be very good at it.

National Home Education Research Institute president Brian Ray states,

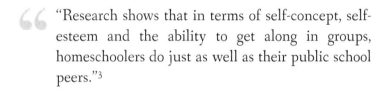

> "Research shows that in terms of self-concept, self-esteem and the ability to get along in groups, homeschoolers do just as well as their public school peers."[3]

He goes on to quote the results of the July 2000 study by the Seattle-based Discovery Institute in which "counselors watched videotapes of homeschooled and schooled children. The counselors, who did not know which children were from each category, noted that the homeschool students demonstrated fewer behavioral problems than their peers." Ray attributes these findings, in part, to the primary role models of homeschoolers,

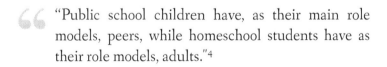

> "Public school children have, as their main role models, peers, while homeschool students have as their role models, adults."[4]

I met a Professor from Austin Pea University in Clarksville, TN. She had written two Periodical Research volumes on the subject of socialization and homeschool, which I read. She quoted similar studies and noted that the homeschool students also worked better across diverse age groups and formed friendships more quickly. This is because they are not limited to peer groups of their chronological year, which happens in most school settings.

Dr. Thomas Smedley of Radford University in Virginia

> "believes homeschoolers have superior socialization skills, and his research supports this claim. He conducted a study in which he administered the Vineyard Adaptive Behavior Scales test to identify mature and well-adapted behaviors in children. Home learners ranked in the 84th percentile, compared to publicly schooled students who were drastically lower in the 23rd."[5]

"Kenneth Bernstein, a high school government and social studies teacher in Prince George's County, Maryland, says that while some homeschool students possess a maturity that their peers lack, others can be sheltered, especially when it comes to exchanging ideas with people from diverse backgrounds:

> "It depends upon how their parents approached [homeschooling]. It also depends upon circumstances other than schooling for the opportunity to interact with young people different from themselves."[6]

And, of course, Mr. Bernstein's comments make perfect sense. The more diversity a person is exposed to the more experience they have to draw from. But the takeaway is that socialization is not weakness for the majority of homeschooled children; rather, it is often a strength.

School as a Socializing Agent

Public school is a valuable institution to assure that education is available to everyone. I have no problem paying taxes to help provide the service. But at the same time we have to remember that schools are not just teaching academic skills. As the main societal socializing agent, they are transmitting cultural values and norms as part of that socialization. All education has a world-view, a foundational set of beliefs determining the perspective from which the material is taught. It is very important to know what our public school's philosophies are as they deeply influence much more than one might realize at first glance.

Being government institutions, our public school's values and norms have to represent all of our country's varied beliefs and serve all of the population. When you really think about that it is an impossible task for every mindset to be equally represented, especially when many of the varied viewpoints are actually contradictory. Ravi Zacharias, a well-known apologist says it this way,

 "All-inclusive philosophies can only come at the cost of truth."[7]

It may sound good to be "tolerant" of all and to "just get along," but in the practical sense, Zacharias notes it is impossible.

As parents, Brett and I care deeply what values, ethics and absolutes are taught, and we don't agree with everything the pluralistic school system deems true in these areas. That conflict in belief caused us to question the potential negative influence school could have on our children as the main socializing agent it is intended to be. If our children were schooled publicly, they would spend a lot of time immersed in the varied ideologies the school supported and couldn't help but be impacted by them.

Homeschooling provided the opportunity for us to know and manage what philosophies were taught to our children along with the academic skills.

Negative Socialization

Just as a homeschooled student can be sheltered in a way that affects their socialization negatively, a public school environment can expose students to conditions that negatively affect their socialization. Consider the following claim,

> "the mass socialization conducted within schools has brought about a proliferation of delinquent behavior within this nation's youth, reports education researcher, Dr. Michael Slavinski. He notes that student bodies are increasingly riddled with violence, drugs, promiscuity, emotional disorders, crime, contempt for authority, desperate behavior, illiteracy and peer dependency - just to name a few. Today, parents are not as surprised to see reports of fifth-graders having sex in class; hear about school shootings; find drugs or condoms in backpacks; receive phone calls from the police and principals; or witness defiant, apathetic and unrecognizable tones in their children's voices."[8]

And finally,

> "when the Direct Observation Form of the Child Behavior Checklist was administered by education researcher Dr. Larry Shyers to identify 97 problematic behaviors in two groups of children, traditionally schooled students exuded eight times

as many antisocial traits than their homeschooled counterparts."[9]

What About Being a Witness?

Some people argue that Christians should send their children to public school to be a witness or to help support those who are underprivileged. But a person cannot be a witness for something they do not know. Children need to first be taught what is right and true before they can share and defend it. Secondly, children are not the authority in the school environment. They are subject to the governing principles and bound by the same restrictions as their teachers (see Appendix III & IV). There are many more effective ways to reach out and support others without putting our children in compromising circumstances that could ultimately lead to their harm. Again, having said that, if you sense the Lord leading you toward public education, then by all means, do it. But do it with a plan, knowing the risks, and being watchful for where your values are being contradicted or undermined.

Socialization Through Homeschooling

In conclusion, socialization can be successfully accomplished through homeschooling. Considering that negative socialization can be a product of the public school system, we need to carefully weigh all factors when considering our children's education.

I have included in the Appendix a more thorough discussion of how our pluralistic culture impacts the socialization process in the public school system (Appendix I, Pluralism and Socialization), as well as how public school became the norm in the United States (Appendix II, Compulsory Public Education). In Appendix III, I have also included a number of Supreme Court decisions that limit and restrict what values can be taught in the public schools. And, finally, in Appendix IV, I have included a number of resolutions of the National Education Association (NEA), "the nation's largest professional employee organization [which is] committed to advancing the cause of public education"[10] to point out some of the prevailing humanistic philosophies in public education.

As far as cultural socialization is concerned, the secular relativism of the public school system may not be the socialization parents want for their children. Once again, homeschool students do not suffer from the lack of skills to socially interact with others across the age spectrum, so there is no need to worry when faced with the question, "But what about socialization?"

Before we move into some more practical questions and encouragement regarding homeschooling I want to address some thoughts on the purpose of education. Clarifying the purpose will help us keep our schooling goals and focus on track.

THE PURPOSE OF EDUCATION

" Aristotle defined education as the "means of transmission of the accumulated knowledge of a society." G. K. Chesterton states it as "simply [how] the soul of a society passes from one generation to another."

What is the purpose of education? At first glance the answer to this question may appear obvious. We think of basic skills like reading, writing and arithmetic. Or considering the previous chapter discussion, education aids in socialization. In a broader sense we might point out that it promotes equality and opportunity.

But for most, when we talk about our children's education (k-12) it is with an eye towards what it will produce, usually starting with it being a door to a college education, which will lead to a good job, money, and the good life: the American dream. JP Moreland states in his book, *Love Your God With All Your Mind*, "that if you ask most why college is important according to various studies, increasing numbers of college freshmen, on the advice of their parents, say their primary goal in going to college is to get a good job and ensure a secure financial future for themselves. This parallels a trend in the same students toward valuing a good job more than developing a meaningful philosophy of life."[1]

When education is limited to standardized results the beauty of the individual gets lost. Yet, since education is largely driven by college preparation, almost as soon as children become school aged they begin being weighed and measured by the state standards and expectations. I've had numerous conversations with parents of children from elementary to high school who were falsely assured or fearfully threatened by their child's GPA—as if it is the ultimate measure of success. GPA's represent only a small portion of what a child has learned and who they are overall.

I recently spoke at a number of homeschool conferences in Asia. While in Singapore, a man who had taught in their schools stated that their system is extremely competitive toward the goal of higher education, making their process very test-driven. Each student's path to success is determined by how well they do on the national exams. He lamented how this has hurt the objective of education. He noted how it affected all areas, even music:

"It used to be that students would take piano to learn to play the instrument. They enjoyed the development of their skills and creativity through the learning process. Now they find out what the song is for the test that year and only practice it in order to pass the test. The value of playing the piano has been lost."

In many ways America's public education system is doing the

same—making university entrance the goal at the cost of real learning and personal development.

While the academic path is certainly worthy of consideration, there are many other benefits of education that will be missed if we become preoccupied with the assessment of our children's academic performance. Surely, God had more in mind when He created each of us. So it's important to question cultural education mindsets in order to determine which facets restrict our children't growth, and which ones enhance it.

For example, not everyone is college bound, and many who do begin, don't finish. Statistically, "as many as 1 in 3 first-year [college] students won't make it back for sophomore year."[2] But everyone will live in society, and their character will influence the whole for better or worse.

With statistics by the 2017 Census Bureau stating that 66.6% of the population is not completing college, we do our children a disservice if we spend twelve years of their life focused too narrowly on the goal of college entry and the promise of great return from a degree. I've read numerous articles about Millennials expressing frustration at not having found the fulfillment promised from their careers, and it is confusing to them. One article quotes Cal Newport, a professor at Georgetown University, stating that in the last 20 years "the phrase 'a secure career' has gone out of style, just as the phrase 'a fulfilling career' has gotten hot."[3] A career is only part of a person's life, can change often, and is not guaranteed to be the most fulfilling part at that. But a meaningful philosophy is what will aid in finding the fulfillment we seek. Knowing who you are, being grounded and principled, will serve you in every facet of life.

In his book, *Norms and Nobility*, David Hicks says,

 "Not everyone is obliged to excel in philosophy, medicine, or law, nor are all equally favored by nature but all are destined to live in society and to practice virtue."[4]

The bigger picture of education then, whether it includes college or not, is "the cultivation of the human spirit: to teach the young to know what is good, to serve it above self, reproduce it, and to recognize that in knowledge lies this responsibility."[5]

Education for the sake of knowledge is not an end in itself; true education reaches beyond the means of acquiring knowledge for a specific goal to instill in the individual a sense of obligation to serve and benefit others, because "in knowledge lies this responsibility." In short, the goal of true education is to acquire both knowledge and character, for knowledge without character is self-serving; whereas, knowledge with character considers how we might use what we know to benefit others. I like what Martin Luther King, Jr. adds,

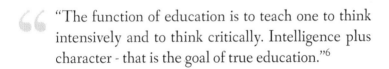

"The function of education is to teach one to think intensively and to think critically. Intelligence plus character - that is the goal of true education."[6]

So then, the multifaceted product of education includes intellectual skills and character development. Intellectual skills are defined as the ability to learn, process ideas and concepts, and communicate them. It is equipping students with tools and confidence so that they can approach any subject or endeavor and have the intellectual abilities to tackle it. And character, which we'll look at next, enables us to steward wisely what we know in a way that contributes to the well being of others.

As stated, the growth of academic skills is only part of the foundation. The second part, character development (tempering and maturing), focuses the attention on a person's philosophy of life, which will guide how they use their skills. Character comes from not only studying God's world but His Word, and then intentionally persevering in the application of its principles to our lives. Everyone has a philosophy of life. But many are not aware of their perspective or deliberate about fashioning what they are aware of into that which pleases God. They have gathered pieces of ideas along the way, so their philosophy has been caught rather than produced through humble reflection, revelatory insight and perseverance in application. The deliberate development of what we believe and why we believe it (knowing ourselves and matching our actions with our confession), form our sense of identity. And out of the process of persevering in our growing understanding of what we know to be true of God, strong character is fashioned.

Training the mind and tempering the heart together also leads to being outwardly focused, as alluded to by Hicks when he speaks of "practicing virtue," and when he talks about responsibility. So a complete education produces both utility—state of being useful, profitable and beneficial (what you do), and essence —state of quality, principle and core substance (who you are).

Bertrand Russell says, "Education should have two objectives, first, to give definite knowledge: reading and writing, language and mathematics, and so on; secondly, to create those mental habits which will enable people to acquire knowledge and form sound judgements for themselves."[7]

Sound judgement should not be confused with the wrongful judgement of others. Judgement simply means

> "to form an opinion about through careful weighing of evidence and testing of premises."[8]

For judgement to be sound then, we must ensure our opinions are based on ample evidence that has been carefully weighed and tested against an agreed upon standard. For example, Christians are not to judge one another with condemnation, as in, to assume we are better than others or conclude their motive (Romans 8:1, Phil 2:3, 1 Cor 2:11), but we are called to judge the actions of those who profess to follow Jesus (including ourselves) by assessing and challenging the evidence in our lives that does not align with the truth of God's character, will and ways (1 Cor. 5:12, 6:1-5, Gal 6:1). So we must grow the ability to rightly evaluate and weigh situations, claims and products in the light of what we know to be true about God.

We want our children to assess and judge rightly, with the goal of their being able to effectively govern themselves; a mission only truly accomplished once they are securely and confidently grounded in truth. The process of acquiring knowledge and the skills necessary for careful, critical thinking trains the mind and instills the information, ideals and values worth preserving (socialization). Many educational efforts end here. Education falls short if our only goal is the acquisition of academic knowledge. A student can be really smart, yet have no character. And remember Lincoln's wisdom,

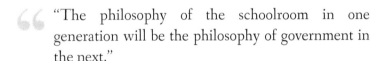

"The philosophy of the schoolroom in one generation will be the philosophy of government in the next."

Our goal is that, by balancing academics with clear, intentional focus on character development, our children will impact society in the most positive way possible in whatever they choose to do. And we will do the same for having taught them.

I had to fight to not compare my children or our homeschooling process to the state standards. It was a challenge to not get caught up in the fear that they or I was not good enough (see Section 2) while remaining focused on our goal. Our current educational culture's social agenda keeps adding more and more demands at the cost of more and more time. I had to guard against falling into the trap for both my children and myself to perform. Homeschooling allows some relief from those demands, because parents can be deliberate with their time and keep their educational purpose clearly in view.

Our children's skills will be directed by their character, which translates not only to their profession or vocation but to all roles they will play in society: spouse, parent, citizen, friend. When we rightly focus on the fact that we are "cultivating the spirit" and "intelligence plus character" it allows our children to become who God created them to be. They were born for this time, and through a well-rounded education we want them to become spiritually mature because "a spiritually mature person is a wise person. And a wise person has the savvy and skill necessary to lead an exemplary life and to address the issues of the day in a responsible, attractive way that brings honor to God."[9]

That is the aim for our children, and for us. Articulating the purpose of education clearly like this helps us balance all the noise and distractions and use our time wisely. It causes us to reflect on what we believe is worth instilling in our children and navigate where and how to best accomplish that. Considering the purpose of education in this light, parents are excellent prospects for teaching their children and homeschooling is a great venue in which to do it.

∿

Section 2

DOUBTS, QUESTIONS AND FEARS

"The journey of a thousand miles begins with a single step."

Lao Tzu

4

AM I ENOUGH?

W hen our daughter Laurén was five years old, many of my friends who had kindergarten aged children decided they were going to homeschool. As I said, though my husband and I had considered homeschooling and thought there were numerous advantages, I wasn't convinced that I wanted to do it, or that I could do it. Some of my immediate fears and concerns were, what if we tried it and didn't like it? Would my children be able to rejoin the system? Would homeschooling put them at a disadvantage if they wanted to go to public school later on? What about college? Would I somehow limit their options if we homeschooled?

Additionally, could I really teach our children all they needed to know so they would have all the opportunities public school students have available?

I was a terrible student when I was in school. Could I really handle tough subjects like math and science? What about having multiple children at different ages and levels at the same time; how do you manage them time-wise, grade-wise? How could I possibly teach them all effectively? What about the wonderful shared experiences of high school like sports, prom and social clubs? Do I want them to miss out on those memories? All these unknowns made my head hurt.

Finally, just because many of my friends were homeschooling, was that enough reason for me to do it? I didn't want to join a passing fad. Our children's education was too important to haphazardly go against the grain without really weighing the potential long-term costs. Remember, it was the late 90's, so although homeschooling was legal it was still in the very infant stages. As stated earlier, there were very few books on the subject, only a handful of curricula available, and not many students that had been homeschooled to test how they fared against their peers.

Over the years, I have talked to numerous parents who echoed these concerns and questions about homeschooling, especially the fear that they didn't think they were enough. I just recently met a woman with grown children and, as we were talking about our lives, the discussion of homeschooling came up. She said,

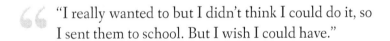

> "I really wanted to but I didn't think I could do it, so I sent them to school. But I wish I could have."

As I listened to her, my heart broke because I know she could have homeschooled. I silently thanked God, because I resonated with her fears; had the Lord not encouraged me, I would have been the one speaking those words of regret today. It made me all the more determined to write this book so that not another parent will say no to homeschooling simply because they think they can't do it.

Like this woman, and many others, my biggest struggle was my awareness of my own limitations causing me to ask the question, "Am I enough?"

You Are Stupid

66 "You are stupid!"

Exasperated with me one day in class, those are the words my third grade teacher spoke over me. I don't remember the situation that provoked the comment. I only remember the comment. I was afraid it was true; I was stupid because very early on in school, I realized I was not making the mark. The other students were faster and better able to produce what the teacher wanted. So when she said it out loud, I received it. From that day on I believed I was stupid and tried to cover my weaknesses, which of course only made matters worse. When I graduated from high school, my GPA was too low to get into university. I had failed geometry and french and barely passed algebra and English. I was able to take twelfth grade over at the community college and then transfer into university after that. But I still needed help. I got through college with the help of my parents, by making friends with good students and by praying and seeing God perform miracles on my behalf!

I kid you not! My biology exam, which was comprised of five essays based on very specific notes we had taken in class, was a perfect example. I remember studying very hard, but when I turned over the test and glanced at the first essay question, though I could visualize the pages in my notebook that the information was on, I couldn't remember it. So I prayed for mercy. Just then the fire alarm went off and the professor said, "It is now an open book test! Bring it back next class." I got an A! But I digress...

The point is I was a very weak student! (My third grade teacher confirmed it!) Okay, she was wrong, I wasn't stupid, but I was deficient in scholastic skills. And here we were as a family now embarking on a journey where I would be the primary teacher for our children. It was a scary prospect to bare this responsibility. Realistically, how long could I actually success-fully teach our children, especially with my own obvious academic weaknesses?

Are You Enough? Yes and No!

Are you enough? Yes you are! And no, you're not! How's that for a clear answer? Before I answer the Yes! part and share my growth as a homeschooling parent to help you see that you are indeed enough, I want to share with you a revelation I had about "not being enough" that changed my homeschooling perspective. I am sorry to say it came many years into my journey, but, hope-fully, this will resonate with you and you will be able to see the truth of it as you begin.

When we began homeschooling we felt we were to commit on a year-to-year basis. I felt the weight of the children's educa-tion. Brett was very committed to our decision and was therefore fully supportive and encouraging toward me. But, because I was doing the majority of the daily teaching and managing, I strug-gled with continuing as I was so aware of my weaknesses and shortcomings.

I would beg God to compensate for me and empower me to carry out the task. Each year I would struggle with questioning whether the children would be better off in school. God would faithfully answer my cry and encourage us to continue on. So I would commit for the next year and then the cycle would repeat the following year. It was nerve racking to say the least.

Then one year, while I was struggling through the regular roller coaster of emotions, God moved miraculously on our behalf and Laurén got accepted into a one day a week homeschool academy. (Actually, this wasn't the first time He moved miraculously on our behalf during our homeschool journey, but it was the moment I finally had an epiphany!) I had heard about the academy when we first moved to Maryland but it was full. The program was amazing, but there was a waiting list that was a number of years long. I forgot about it until almost the end of that first year, and then one day on a "whim" called and made an appointment. We were scheduled for an interview the following Monday. After our meeting, the principal of the program encouraged us to get our application and paperwork in by Thursday that same week because the board was gathering for the last admission meeting of the year, and sometimes a student would be accepted and bypass the waiting list. There were no guarantees, but it was worth a try. He encouraged us to go to the orientation for the classes the following week, even if we didn't get in, to gain a better understanding of what they offered.

So we did just that. When we walked into the orientation there was an envelope on the welcome table with Laurén's name on it. She had been accepted. I cried! The whole process was truly a miracle: from the fact that I even thought about the academy when I did and followed through with a call, that we got an appointment before the final enrollment decisions were to be made, to attending the orientation and being accepted at that point because it gave us full access to the classes being offered for the upcoming school year.

When I reflected on God's miraculous goodness to us, from His guiding us to where we needed to be without my even really knowing what we needed, to His directing the timing and our steps right through the process of enrollment, I had a revelation: I had been looking at homeschooling all wrong. I had seen it as something I wanted to do for my children, therefore, the weight of its success was on my abilities, my research, my efforts. But as I realized there was no way in my own strength or skill I could have orchestrated the events of the last couple of weeks to open the door for this academy, I began to remember all the other miracles God had done on behalf of our family over the years so that we could homeschool successfully up to that point. He had led us to books and co-ops and other homeschooling families. He had provided extra income and programs and resources that we would somehow stumble across at just the right time. I was overcome with the reality of His faithfulness to compensate for my weaknesses by the way He led and guided us. And for the first time I understood that homeschooling was His idea for our children, not mine. Rather, I was the instrument through which He had chosen to accomplish His will. That was why the most unlikely, struggling student (me) would be enough to homeschool her children; because it didn't all depend on her! God had considered my weaknesses! He knew my limitations only too well!

 "But God choose the foolish things of the world to shame the wise; He choose the weak to shame the strong" 1 Corinthians 1:27 (NIV).

I needed to trust Him. I needed His strength! And through my dependence on Him, He was going to accomplish something beautiful. I got to be a part of the work He was doing but now knew, beyond a shadow of a doubt, it was only by His grace.

I also saw more clearly that God was ordering the steps of our children for His purpose. It was His will for them to be homeschooled as part of who He was shaping them to be! Up until then, when it came to homeschooling, I saw the pattern more like God reaching them through me, rather than Him reaching to them directly; I was only one of many instruments He was using. However, in the Kingdom, remember, there are no grandchildren, only children. In that way, children need their own personal relationship with God and cannot be saved through someone else's relationship with Him. Likewise, He is working out the details of their lives, like He does for everyone, to equip them and shape them for their future and His glory. A future only He knows. Honestly, it was a holy moment! Based on that, I committed to homeschooling without excuse until or unless God revealed a different path for our family. I decided to change my confession and no longer bemoan my limitations and fears, but to confess God's purpose and power.

What a glorious day that was! My attitude changed, my commitment changed, my purpose changed, my hope changed. God gave me vision!

If I could give you anything it would be the deposit of faith God gave me that day! I would ask Him to open your eyes so you can see His provision, just like he opened the eyes of the servant of Elisha:

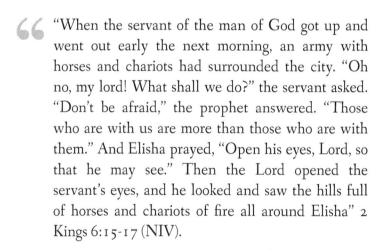

"When the servant of the man of God got up and went out early the next morning, an army with horses and chariots had surrounded the city. "Oh no, my lord! What shall we do?" the servant asked. "Don't be afraid," the prophet answered. "Those who are with us are more than those who are with them." And Elisha prayed, "Open his eyes, Lord, so that he may see." Then the Lord opened the servant's eyes, and he looked and saw the hills full of horses and chariots of fire all around Elisha" 2 Kings 6:15-17 (NIV).

The Lord surrounds us too. He is so good! If you haven't yet received that confidence in homeschooling that He can do this through you, would you be willing to take a moment now and ask Him to give it to you? Then, when He does, write it down and put the date on it! Then put it somewhere you will see it often to remind you that this is God's will for your family at this time. You are not on this journey alone; God will empower, lead and direct you. I can't tell you how often I sensed the leading of the Lord in something and started with confidence. But then, when I hit the first glitch, I'd bail! But I learned to refocus on the vision, pick up where I got discouraged or derailed, and get back on track! Having that vision and going back to it often helped me tremendously. Hopefully, it will help you too. So the answer to the question, Am I enough? is - NO! You are not enough. But, with God - YES! You are MORE than enough!

The rest of this section will address the most common doubts, fears and questions parents face when considering homeschooling. I will also share some practical applications of my family and other families on how we walked the process out day to day.

I'M NOT AN EXPERT

Most people are comfortable teaching young children. We are confident regarding simple math and basic reading because we can read and add. But we are afraid of homeschooling as our children get older because of what we don't know or remember. We think that a good teacher needs to be an expert, someone who knows all the answers. But the truth is, that is not what makes a good teacher. What makes a good teacher is one who is willing to grow. Classical Conversations, a homeschool organization, explains this concept by using the term, Lead Learner.

Lead Learner

Lead Learner implies that you don't know everything at the start but that you are willing to learn and grow as you go. I love that! It's so freeing. Our public education system promotes the expert model, which assumes you must be an authority on a subject and that expertise is what qualifies you to teach. I am not against growing to be an expert, but I am against the philosophy that you have nothing to offer until you are an expert.

The concept of teaching or leading learning centers on the ability to figure out what needs to be taught and effectively communicate that information, thereby allowing a parent to start where they are and grow in the education process with their student. And, contrary to the expert teacher idea, parents are doing an excellent job teaching their children. "Homeschool students score above average on achievement tests regardless of their parents' level of formal education or their family's household income. Whether homeschool parents were ever certified teachers is not related to their children's academic achievement."[1]

There are so many resources available today to help a parent navigate. It is okay to not know it all when you start. John Maxwell says, "The reality is that you will never get much done unless you go ahead and do it before you are ready."[2] That has definitely been true of my journey! I didn't know it all and honestly, I am still learning. But I did try to utilize the available resources; I encourage you to do so as well. Talk to experienced homeschool parents; go to curriculum fairs and conferences. Choose a curriculum and begin. You will grow as you go!

Grow as You Go

I remember when Laurén was four, Brooks was two and I was pregnant with Pierz. Some homeschooling friends, whose children were in the sixth grade, had been attending a math class once a week at a local co-op. The person who was leading the class had to quit and my friends asked me if I would take over teaching math once a week to their two children. I would introduce the concepts to the students and then they would do the work at home. I looked at the textbook; it was Saxon 7/6 (a commonly used, 6th/7th grade, homeschool math curriculum). It looked a little challenging but we could use the additional income, so I said yes! (You will see this is a pattern in my life. When I am faced with an opportunity that seems beyond what I can do, but it pays—I try!)

Well, it turned out to be a good job. The students did well and I was able to lead them. There were more than a few times that I had to work through the instruction part to make sure I understood what I was teaching them. I remember thinking, if I did homeschool Laurén and 7/6 was challenging for me now, what would I do about higher level math? What about Pre-algebra and Algebra?

Fast forward six years to the summer before Laurén was to start Saxon 7/6, I was terrified! I was about to enter the section of math that I feared most! But surprisingly, that year was not at all as difficult as I had anticipated.

You see, I hadn't considered the personal equipping I would receive before we reached that milestone. By that time, I had done kindergarten math three times, first and second grade math two times and third through fifth grade math one time; so I was extremely prepared for Saxon 7/6. Interestingly, today, I am a math tutor. I tutor Algebra I, Algebra II, Geometry or Pre-Calculous almost every day after school and have for many years! When someone requests tutoring for their sixth grade child (Saxon 7/6 level), I almost feel guilty charging them because the content is now so easy and, believe it or not, fun! But the point is, I grew with my children and you will too. And, as the Lead Learner, you also get to use the teacher's guide, which is a big help.

If you pull your students out of public schools when they are older, or you hit some higher level subjects that you just can't or don't want to put in the time to learn, there are options. In that case hire a tutor, or have your child take a class through a co-op. I like to think of myself as managing my children's education, and there is no shame in using outside resources to accomplish it. But most likely, when that time comes, just like me you will be able to handle those difficult subjects that scare you now. I never thought I would be teaching higher level math. Nor did I think I would be teaching Biology and leading dissections. And I certainly didn't think I would enjoy it if I did! But I am, and I do!

Personal Side Product

By being engaged in the learning process along with my children there was also a side product that I didn't expect: I grew tremendously and redeemed my own education. As I said, I am now a tutor (for public school and homeschool students) and there is not a subject I have been asked to teach that I've not been able to do successfully.

On occasion, parents have requested that I tutor subjects I did not yet feel competent to teach. In instances like that, I simply tell them that I am willing to try and if they are okay with me only being a few weeks ahead of their student, I would tutor them. I also explained that if I found I couldn't do a good job, I would let them know so they could find someone else who could. Most of the time the parents didn't mind, they were just so thankful someone was willing to help their student. But, I have not yet ever had to tell someone that they need to hire a different tutor. I have always been able to learn the material and tutor their student.

This is due partly to relearning along with my children and partly to the fact that I have learned how to learn. I thought a person was either born smart and did well in school or they were born stupid and did poorly in school. But I have learned there is an art to learning. It may take some people longer to learn certain skills than others. But in most cases, with persistence, a person can learn anything they are willing to put forth the effort to learn.

Today, I know I am far from stupid. I understand that I just needed more help and time to learn than many of my peers. I wish I had known that in school!

Now, for the record, since I got better at homeschooling as time went on, I have been tempted to feel badly for our oldest daughter, Laurén! If I were to begin homeschooling today, I would do some things differently with her, or at least I think I would. But I have to remind myself that I was who I was at the time, and God was faithful. If I had waited until I had it all together, I would still be waiting. I had no choice but to jump in.

I love this quote by John Maxwell: "Growing can be messy business. It means admitting you don't have the answers. It requires making mistakes. It can make you look foolish. Most people don't enjoy that. But that is the price of admission if you want to improve."[3] I definitely made my share of mistakes! But I was faithful to teach my children every school day to the best of my ability, and the Lord was faithful to direct their steps and compensate for all our weaknesses. And by the way, Laurén was awarded a number of scholarships in college and tested into honors, for which I praise God.

Either way, I didn't know the art of learning when I was in school or when I began homeschooling, yet God used me anyway. And He will use you too! You will grow with your children, and there is grace for your growth in the process! That has definitely been true of my journey and many of my friends, and it will be true of yours too as you apply yourself and learn to learn. And, when all is said and done, you may very well become the expert!

6

IS PUBLIC SCHOOL ENOUGH?

S ince this book is aimed at the person who is thinking of homeschooling, this chapter focuses on some marked benefits homeschooling provides over a formal school (individualized, family-managed education versus a group, system-managed education) through areas such as one-on-one instruction, consistency, awareness, calendar and schedule management, self discipline and character growth. In the same way we tend to question whether we are enough, we need to question whether public school is enough.

Group Instruction VS Individual Instruction

Individualized teaching provides tremendous benefits over being in a classroom. In a classroom setting the teacher has to focus on the average level of the students in the group. She cannot assure that everyone understands the concept being taught before moving to the next concept. In math, for example, the first six weeks are usually dedicated to reviewing the material from the previous year. The remaining chapters and concepts are then divided into time frames in order to cover the required material in a timely manner over the course of the school year. The chapter divisions are based on the curriculum, not the students. So if a student is ahead, they will be stuck working on a concept regardless of their ability and, likewise, if a student is behind the class will move on to the next concept regardless of their comprehension of the material.

Homeschooling provides the flexibility to adjust and consider the individual or family. Of our three children, Laurén struggled the most with math. I remember in second and third grade, since she was very quick with computation but labored with telling time and money, I was able to decide how much time we would spend on each chapter. The first few chapters in second and third grade math covered computation, so I tested Laurén at the beginning of each year to see what she had retained. This allowed us to cover the review material the first week, which was very helpful because we could then spend more time on the concepts that were difficult for her. This was a huge benefit.

I will discuss our middle child's struggles in more detail later in the chapter, but I am so thankful that we were able to set the progression of his education to the more slow and steady pace he needed and not be pushed by the arbitrary speed of the school system. He was behind grade level for the majority of his life. Had he attended public school he would have been wrongly labeled, frustrated and held back because he did not learn at the pace the school system set. The flexibility of one-on-one learning allowed him to keep moving forward while addressing the areas he needed to be successful.

Some people argue that the structure of a group classroom setting and the authority of an adult other than the parent is an important benefit of public or private school education. In homeschooling, we also participate in structured, other adult-lead environments and group learning settings, so the skills mentioned above are actually acquired. The difference is that those settings are not providing the dominant structure. I have found that the dual experience of one-on-one instruction and group settings broadens the student's abilities.

Consistency

Another advantage of homeschooling is consistency in your children's curriculum and instruction. Having been their teacher the previous year, and working one-on-one with them, you have a clear understanding of what was taught, so you can easily build upon that the following year without any gaps. In a public school system, you are less likely to have knowledge of these variables. Additionally, a lot can change from year to year: teachers change, curriculums change, schools change. These changes can create gaps in learning of which you may be unaware. But, as a homeschooling parent, because you are in charge of the curriculum decision and involved in its usage, you will have a clear knowledge of what your child has covered and how well they mastered it the year before. While gaps can happen in the home environment as well, they are less likely because this knowledge equips you to better control consistency in your child's learning.

I was aware of concepts and content in every subject we studied and was able to build on that. This is especially helpful if you switch curriculums. One year I switched curriculum in language arts. The new curriculum assumed my child knew certain concepts. When she expressed confusion, I wasn't worried because I knew which parts we had and hadn't covered. So I was able to take a few days and teach the preliminary concepts in order to continue successfully with the new curriculum.

Another time the consistency homeschooling allows was

made evident was when we moved from Tennessee to Maryland. Our children didn't miss a beat in their education, as all of their schooling moved with us; so there was no disruption in any curriculum. There was also a side benefit I hadn't considered. Since our school moved with us, we were able to maintain our daily routine, which brought a sense of familiarity. Having our schedule at home be the same in Maryland as it was in Tennessee helped the children acclimate more easily, thereby making a huge move a much smoother transition.

Awareness

One-on-one instruction keeps the student engaged and focused (or at least the teacher knows if the student is engaged or focused!). In a classroom, a student could be daydreaming the whole time, and if they are a naturally quiet person the teacher may not notice. That was part of my problem in public school. I was a well-behaved child so my issues were missed. In home-schooling you will know right away if your child is missing a concept or if they are not paying attention! This is valuable because it means you will know if the allotted time is being used effectively or wasted by whether your child has finished their work or not.

This brings us to the problem of children getting their work done! I will cover this in more detail later on in the book, but for now I want to share some great insight a wise, experienced educator, who was also a homeschooling father, gave me when I was struggling with my children's seemingly absent attention span! He told me that most people have a few days a month when they are not as productive. He said to give both myself and my children grace in this area, as there will be days where not much is accomplished by me or them. That was very helpful advice. That way the occasional unproductive day didn't make me feel like a failure. If we aren't aware of the fact that we all have a few off days in any given month, we can have unrealistic expectations for our children, and ourselves. Without it, we can wrongfully expect them to be fully engaged at all times and frustrated if that is not the case. The reality is there will be focused days and unfocused days.

Being aware of what is accomplished daily is a benefit of homeschooling as you are on top of how much learning is and isn't taking place.

Calendar and Schedule

In a school system, the government or board determines the schedule. They determine what time you start and finish each day. They determine when days off will be. They determine holidays. They determine rules regarding sick days. Homeschooling and its individualized focus lets you determine when you will start, when you will finish, what days will be off and when and for how long holidays will be. You will need to comply with the approximate 180 days rule in elementary school and the 120 hours required per credit in high school (double-check your state for compliance), but otherwise, homeschooling gives your family wonderful flexibility. Throughout our years of homeschooling, we have been able to prioritize the things that matter most to us including trips, family time, church and related events, ballet lessons, sports, special projects and so on (we took a month off to write, record, produce and edit a professional music video during our middle son's sophomore year), and still accomplished the required instruction.

Discipline and Character

When you homeschool, your children most likely will challenge your authority as Teacher, whereas those same children may not openly challenge a public/private school teacher. Often times, when I have told people I homeschool, the parent will respond by saying something like, "I could never do that. My child and I would kill each other!" I understand the reality they're talking about. But there is an assumption in that statement I want to address. The idea is that by putting your willful child in school the parent avoids the battle (and for a while they might). But I would caution parents not to assume it means they have resolved the issue.

Something I have learned is that my children's character flaws do not simply dissipate with time. You can wrongly believe an issue has been dealt with when it may actually be lying dormant. Along with their strengths and our dreams of all we hope for them to become, it is imperative that we also learn to see our children's flaws. Sometimes we make excuses for them when we need to instead acknowledge their weakness and make them take responsibility. I confess, I learned both of these lessons the hard way. I learned that, not only do character flaws need to be addressed, it may take much longer to work though them than the averages presented in parenting books!

Homeschooling involves training the character, and you will need to address and discipline those character flaws directly regardless of what form of education you choose. If you don't they will only surface later on. And, honestly, they only become more and more difficult to work through as the child grows older, and bigger! It's always best to begin the process early on, setting the standard according to God's directives, and then begin helping the child to understand how they actually honor Him as they honor the standards, and you. We will look at this more closely in Chapter 12.

Character and discipline are a problem for the school system too.

> "We have gone from a time when parents believed what the teacher said in regards to their child's behavior and reacted accordingly, to the present where parents stare in disbelief and think of a million excuses as to why their child misbehaves,"

says Marybeth Harrison, a public school speech therapist in Hunterdon County, N.J. She said teachers are

> "sadly the first to be blamed," as parents cite poor classroom management or a lack of patience. "It's time for parents to start parenting and teach manners, respect, etc. ... at home. Let teachers teach."[1]

Our children have sinful natures and there is no getting around having to deal with them. Teaching them to respect and submit to parental authority is a necessary part of parenting, and homeschooling naturally forces us to face that. Also keep in mind that the environment in many public schools may even encourage rebellion or disrespect because the teacher's authority is limited.

There is no perfect system, but in the areas of one-on-one instruction, consistency, awareness, scheduling, discipline and character development, homeschooling has some significant advantages.

Even so, some parents may still hesitate to homeschool because of the possibility that their circumstance could change at some point, or the fear that they simply might not like homeschooling. What then? They wonder, "Is it possible for my child to switch to the public school system?" The simple answer is, yes; they can enter or re-enter the local school system fairly easily.

Switching Between School Systems

Typically through eighth grade, regardless of academic achievement, children can enter the public school system in the grade they would be according to their age. This is true in most states. So if you homeschooled until your child was ten years old and then went to the government school, she would enter as a fifth grader. I have known numerous students who have entered public school after homeschooling (and those that have started homeschooling after many years in the public school). There is an adjustment period for students on both sides of the coin. Usually though, for the homeschool student acclimating to public school the struggle is not with the academic part of school but more with the adjustments necessary in acclimating to school life.

I asked a former student from our co-op about her adjustment to government high school from homeschooling. She said, "Public school is way harder!" I was surprised because the homeschool curriculum we use is quite rigorous, so I asked her to explain.

"Well, first of all I have to get up at 6:00 AM every day. Then my classes are really long and it is hard to stay awake and pay attention. Then I have homework at night. When I was homeschooled I got all my work done before dinner."

Oh, I said, "But what about the school work. Is it harder?"

"Oh, no, the work is easy!"

I had to laugh.

In other cases, some students have found being a part of a large classroom an adjustment, and not having the one-on-one help created a new challenge.

Presently, with Common Core standards being relatively

new, there could be additional factors that might affect the transition, time will tell. But students generally seem to transition just fine. The point is, you can change your mind and your children can enter public school. But keep in mind that government schools have their own weaknesses, and not all children fare well there. Beyond that, not all challenges with students going from homeschooling to public or private school are due to them having been homeschooled. The individual strengths and weaknesses of the child also factor in.

As stated, a student who is in first through eighth grade will typically transition into public school at the grade their age dictates, but after ninth grade a student can have more challenges, such as losing some of their credits or needing additional ones. Or sometimes it takes a little negotiating. A friend's son entered public high school as a sophomore and it took some back and forth with the school system to justify a few of his freshmen credits. Though it required extra effort, in the end all his credits counted and he entered at his appropriate grade level. Also keep in mind that once a student is sixteen years old they can begin attending most community colleges for some of their classes and receive dual credit, which is another option to consider if you want to enter the system near the end of high school.

If your child is in private or public school and you decide to homeschool, there will be a transition there as well. It will be an adjustment for both you and your child. Keeping that in mind will make those first few months easier. But it is totally doable! I've known lots of students who have successfully transitioned to homeschooling from all grade levels: elementary, junior high and high school.

One caution to consider overall: Homeschooling parents can fear being rejected by the school system down the road so much that they do not fully embrace the homeschooling journey. However, trying to keep one foot in the system in case things don't work out causes a person to be hesitant and to second-guess themselves. I understand because I struggled with this myself until I eventually realized that it's like trying to please two masters, which only creates greater frustration. Should you choose the homeschooling path, I would encourage you to embrace it fully and make the most of every moment. If you decide to enter the system at some point, deal with it then. The point is, if you are faithfully educating your children at home and they enter the public system at some point later on, while there can always be challenges, they should transition just fine.

Struggling Students

What about a student with learning disabilities? Is home-schooling an option for them? Absolutely! Public schools certainly have the resources to help. I tutor a number of students who have IEP's (Individual Education Plan) from their schools, and I deeply respect teachers who have to manage numerous IEP's while maintaining the other requirements and responsibilities in their classroom. But it is exciting to know that for struggling students, homeschooling is still an option. In many ways the one-on-one focus for a child with learning challenges is an advantage. I have known parents who have homeschooled students with Dysgraphia, Dyslexia, Cognitive Delays, Down's Syndrome and Asperger's to name a few. Our son Brooks would have probably needed an IEP had he attended public school.

Brooks is our middle child. He has a pastoral heart, is creative, athletic and funny.

He is also my most compliant child - the only toddler of our three who would wear what I asked him without a fight! He struggled with reading and, consequently, he didn't like to read (I'm not really sure which came first)! But either way he was slow at it. He also struggled with writing; the two skills necessary for most all other subjects! I was extremely conflicted about home-schooling him because I knew just how far behind he was academically.

When Brooks was in the third grade my friend stopped homeschooling and put her children into our neighborhood's elementary school. She told me how well her children were doing and that I should really put Brooks in school too. Her words struck me deeply at the heart level. We felt called to homeschool, yet I knew Brooks was weak and I wanted him to thrive too. I had to work a lot more with Brooks on his schoolwork than I did with the other two. What if he didn't get the academic foundation or skills he needed from me? The last thing I wanted to do was keep him at home if school would be a better place for him. Could I really gamble with his education like that? And the many questions came flooding in. So, one afternoon at the end of his third grade year, I decided to walk around the school grounds and pray once more, asking God if we should put him in school the next year.

Interestingly, a teacher had stayed late that day and noticed me as she was leaving. We began to talk. It turned out she was the third grade teacher! Go figure... so I poured my heart out to her. She asked good questions about Brooks, about what I was teaching and how I was going about it. Then she got quiet and said, "Can I tell you my opinion off the record? I would not send him to school. You are teaching him the right skills and you have the advantage of one-on-one instruction. The public school could not give any more than you are already giving. Plus, by talking to you and hearing you are a Christian, there are a lot of moral issues that we can't address here at school." Then she told me a couple of incidents that had happened recently and encouraged me to keep doing what I was doing. I cried as I walked home. I was so encouraged because, not only had God given me my answer, He actually had it waiting for me before I began walking!

By faith, we kept going.

You would think that things would get better right away. Or at least they would improve reasonably soon. After all, God had given an incredibly direct answer. But Brooks continued to struggle. I remember getting his standardized test results in fifth grade (I often had my kids do standardized tests to get an idea of how they were doing). His scores were below basic in both reading and math. Once again I questioned our choice and once again God, through some specific circumstances, affirmed we were to continue. Though Brooks was improving academically each year, his progress was gradual, and his results were always below average for his age. For example, when he was in fifth grade he was reading at a second grade level. He would improve the next year, but still remain two to three levels behind. And so it went, well into his high school years.

And then, it happened. About half way through his junior year I begin to notice a change. And by his senior year, he was a genius! It was a miracle (that only took 10 years)! Okay, so he wasn't a genius, but Brooks turned the corner, and I was no longer worried. He was actually doing well in both reading and writing. And, wonderfully, along the way he had developed numerous other strengths and skills. Brooks is highly creative and loves video and media. By his junior year he was showing a strong aptitude for video, to the degree that he was already working professionally in his field, so we began praying about whether college was right for him and necessary for his pursuits.

I share that for two reasons. First to acknowledge that not all students are going to be super academics, and that is okay! It is exciting when your child is achieving, and it is devastating when your child is not. But as we pointed out earlier, only 25% of the population actually finishes college. This means that a lot of people are working and holding down good jobs without a degree. And secondly, it demonstrates that Brooks was learning; he was just slower than the norm.

The norms for standardized testing are based on averages to give us markers against a general peer group, but they aren't hard and fast absolutes. Yet, if we are not careful we can treat them as though they are. A person's achievement in the third grade or fifth grade are not determinants of all future success. Brooks' performance being below what the average students his age achieved didn't mean he was destined for failure. But that was a hard thing to keep in focus month after month and year after year when progress was so slow.

It is humbling too. As a parent it is tempting to let your identity be determined by your child's success, or lack thereof. And that is a dangerous stance to take because your focus can easily become their performance, which can inhibit their personal growth and yours. As mentioned, academic learning is certainly important, as are the disciplines involved with hard work. But we must also remember that our goal is to grow the whole person—to love God and others, to value learning, and to develop interpersonal skills and other strengths. I learned that distinction early on, but that didn't mean it wasn't a battle to walk out. Truth is, I was so focused on Brooks' scholastic weakness at times that I totally lost sight of the bigger picture. A doctor's visit during middle school helped bring a fresh perspective.

A Doctor's Insight

Brooks was 12 and suffering from joint pain in his knees, so I took him to the Dr. for a check up. After examining him, she determined there was nothing of concern and pronounced a clean bill of health. Hurray! I was relieved.

She then turned to me and asked. "Where does he go to school?"

Ok, I don't know what it was exactly; maybe it was the very pointed way she looked at me, or the tone of her voice as she asked the question, but I sort of panicked inside.

"Why would she ask that?" I reasoned to myself, "She must have found something else wrong and somehow it is related to my terrible job of homeschooling!" (Panic doesn't always lead to rational thought!) In those earlier years I often felt like I had to defend why I was educating our children at home, especially to strangers, and in that moment I felt I had to defend it to her. So I told her that we homeschooled, but I quickly added, "We test regularly, we are part of a co-op and...."

As I was very animatedly making my case, she held up her hand for me to stop. Then she said,

> "I knew you were doing something differently. I have been a Pediatrician for over 20 years, and I have never seen a boy his age have a relationship with his mother like Brooks has with you."

I was shocked and speechless! (A rare occurrence for me.) I had been so focused on Brooks academically that I had not realized we were reaping other tremendous benefits from homeschooling.

Raising children is not a simple process. People are complex. Life is multifaceted. Remember, you have twelve years of schooling and your goal is to raise the whole person. All our children struggle with something: academics, character, social skills, spirituality. There are no perfect families. Our children will have those struggles regardless of the system of education we choose, and working through them will require patience, consistency and hard work.

In the end, Brooks graduated high school and even ended up going to university (which was a shock! - more on that later). But the point is, I am so grateful that we homeschooled. It was the right choice for him, especially as a struggling student. It was a safe environment and allowed him the time he needed to learn and grow.

If your child is struggling, take heart and know homeschooling could still be the right choice for your family.

COLLEGE, PROM AND RITE OF PASSAGE

College acceptance is another area that parent's often worry will be limited or restricted if they homeschool. Note the following facts from a recent study by the National Home Education Research Institute regarding home-schoolers and college entrance.

> "The home-educated typically score 15 to 30 percentile points above public-school students on standardized academic achievement tests. (The public school average is the 50th percentile; scores range from 1 to 99.) Degree of state control and regulation of homeschooling is not related to academic achievement. Home-educated students typically score above average on the SAT and ACT tests that colleges consider for admissions. Homeschool students are increasingly being actively recruited by colleges."[1]

All our children have been accepted to colleges. In fact, they were accepted to every college they applied to. In the end we chose to start at the community college level and transfer to four year schools for a number of reasons. Two of our children tested into Honors, and the other was walked to the program by a professor after distinguishing himself in his classes. But homeschooled students attend all kinds of colleges and universities for all kinds of reasons, just as their public and private school peers do. I have known homeschool students who have received full academic scholarships, sports scholarships, military scholarships and art scholarships. I know of homeschool students who have gone to state schools and Ivy League schools and many others in between.

An advantage with homeschooling and college applications is that you can find out what the particular college you're interested in looks for in their applicants and adjust your student's high school experience to meet the requirements. Plus, if during high school your child attends a co-op, the learning structure is often similar to the structure of a college class. The students attend the class once a week and then manage their work load during the rest of the time. Learning to work independently and manage their time during the teenage years makes the transition to the academic side of college easier because the format is familiar. And here is a fun fact....

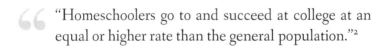

"Homeschoolers go to and succeed at college at an equal or higher rate than the general population."[2]

So, college is definitely as much a potential reality for a homeschool student as it is for any other student.

You Won't Get to Go to Prom!

What about the wonderful shared experiences of high school like sports, prom and clubs? Won't my children miss out on those memories?

We had just met a family at church and were hanging out with them one afternoon at our neighborhood pool. The daughter asked Laurén, who was 12 years old at the time, where she went to school. Laurén answered that she was homeschooled. The girl looked at Laurén sadly and said, "That is too bad; you won't get to go to prom!"

Prom was not even on Laurén's mind at that point, but I remember the statement because it was a concern of mine, too. I am a very social person. Author and preacher Tony Campolo used to share a story about the values in his family and why he was the way he was...a little on the generous side in his weight. He said he used to walk to school with his friend "Johnny," who was very smart. As Johnny was walking out the door each morning, his mother would yell after him, "Johnny! Do you have your books?" But when Tony left for school, his mother would yell, "Tony, do you have your lunch?" He was making the point that those values shaped (no pun intended) the boys' school experience. Johnny was academically successful, and Tony was...well fed! As my children are leaving the house, I always say, "Have fun!" Why? Because social events and activities such as prom, clubs and sports are very important to me! (Now that I think about it, it's a miracle our kids learned anything academic at all!)

Long story short, Laurén was invited by a friend to attend the public school prom and so were both my boys. Truth is, they all went to a couple different proms. They also went to the homeschool prom. Our youngest son, Pierz, along with some of his friends, actually organized a local homeschool prom for both their junior and senior year. They had over 200 students attend! He and his friends ended up being able to go for free, and even made a small profit!

Sports and Clubs

Brooks swam on a club swim team and played on a homeschool football team against private Christian schools. (Homeschool students from both of these organizations have received collegiate swimming and football scholarships.) In some areas homeschool students are able to join local high school sports teams. Laurén danced classical ballet and Pierz took karate. Friends have done everything from horseback riding, 4H, skiing and many other sports. In many countries there is no lack of opportunity for sports and extracurricular actives available for youth, whether public, private or homeschooled. We did pay out of pocket for most of the activities, but school activities usually have out of pocket expenses too. In some situations we received scholarships or the kids helped in various ways to receive discounts.

Again the take away is there are many opportunities for your children and, where they are limited, you can be innovative and organize your own. Pierz and his friends have gained so much more from prom by having taken the leadership for the ones they coordinated. (Plus, the environment at the high school proms they attended compared to the environment of the ones they organized were night and day different. I would choose the home-school prom for my children any day.)

Multiple Children and Ages

As you may know, being a parent of school aged children is hard work! You have to manage a lot regardless of where they go to school. A major advantage of homeschooling is that you have scheduling flexibility the public school can't offer because of their numbers. Some parents use different curriculum for their children, others have different levels of the same curriculum. Some parents combine certain subjects and others use a theme for the year. I have done all of the above. It is not a perfect science. You and your family change and grow, and so do your needs.

For us, the hardest time was when both Laurén and Brooks were school age and Pierz was not. I found it challenging to have quality time with the older children while keeping Pierz occupied (and alive). I did a number of things. I attempted to have Pierz play quietly in the same room. (This did not last very long as he did not understand the concept of "quiet.") I tried letting him play in the other room. (Then if he was quiet, we knew he was probably doing something dangerous or hazardous and that we had better find him!) I had him join us at the table. He would listen or look at a book or color. (This sometimes gave us at least a few minutes) I also had one of the older children play with him while I worked with their sibling, and then they would switch places. (Depending on the day, this would generally create the most uninterrupted teaching time.)

There were also times where I would explain a lesson to Laurén and Brooks and have them work while I played with Pierz. (This would work sometimes, but other times one of the two older children needed supervision and didn't accomplish as much as I hoped.) We would do the harder subjects, the ones where Laurén and Brooks needed my attention most, during Pierz' nap time. This would give us a good couple of hours of uninterrupted time each day. (Unless I was exhausted and needed a nap too!) It is a good idea to try and train the younger children to entertain themselves as well, even if they are in a Pack 'n Play right beside you. Brooks was able to entertain himself at a young age but for Pierz it was more of a challenge. Following are a few ideas to help if you have toddlers.

Practical Ideas for Toddlers

Create a few bins to be used only during school time with items
your toddler can use alongside the other children. Rotate the use
of the boxes depending on your activities.

- Quiet Activities Bin - so they can "do school" at the
  table with the other children. Fill it with items such
  as coloring books, white paper and crayons, sticker
  books and reading books.
- Special Toys Bin - such as puzzles, craft supplies, dry
  erase board. You could rotate the supplies every few
  months to keep it fresh.
- Dress Up Bin - of costumes and accessories, old
  clothes, shoes, boot, hats...
- Music Bin - of instruments or items that make noise.
- Sensory Bin - with Play-Doh, bubbles, containers of
  sand, colored rice or pasta. Other fun sensory
  activities such as letting your toddler stand at the sink
  and play with toys in soapy water can occupy them
  for long periods of time. Obviously, these activities
  are messier and your child will need direct
  supervision.
- Magnet Bin - Magnets on the fridge can be a fun and
  educational activity. Anything from magnetic letters
  and numbers to other picture type magnets will work.
  Sometimes if the magnets are too flat, it is hard for
  little hands to grasp, so keep that in mind when
  choosing items. Again, rotate the magnets.

Another strategy is to categorize activities based on blocks of
time, such as movie-time, music-time, park-time, book-time,
sensory play-time, sibling-time, nap-time, and mommy-time. Of

course, other than mommy-time and nap-time, you wouldn't need to do each one every day, but it gives you a number of ideas to consider rotating through.

A combination of these methods each day allowed us to muddle through the early years. I had to learn that for us homeschooling looked different than your average classroom, and that was okay. Laurén and Brooks had to learn that a quiet and totally structured environment is not always possible. They learned to give grace to each other, to themselves and to me. Honestly, I think this is a positive, natural side effect of homeschooling. You can't always control the environment in the same way a school can control a classroom, which can be frustrating. But that means your family has to learn to consider others in another way. The loud one learns to control themselves for the sake of others and the one that desires structure and quiet has to learn they can't always have it. In the end, homeschooling is a lifestyle. You find a rhythm as a family and, working together, become better people for it.

Finally, it's important to remember that you will not have toddlers forever. It wasn't long before every one of our children had schoolwork to do. One of the advantages was that the boys saw Laurén "doing school" and they wanted to do it too, so they fell more easily into the routine of schooling than she initially did. However you go about it, engaging the early training of toddlers sets the stage for helping our children become life-long learners.

One Child

I had many friends who only had one child and homeschooled. Brooks' best friend was an only child. They do just fine! Also, it's not like you can't have other kids over during the day, attend study groups, play groups, or go to places with other people. I know many parents with multiple children who do all those things. As we grew, we found our routine and flow and found great enjoyment in our many adventures together. So much so that I was actually surprised when we got down to just one child left at home. I always thought it would be sad and lonely with just the two of us, but, to my delight, I loved it! I loved being able to focus on one student, and I think Pierz enjoyed the attention (most of the time). However, I'm also quite certain that he missed his siblings, not because he was lonely, but because he wasn't able to get away with as much when it was only him and me!

Fear Keeps us From Risking

The bottom line is, the question "Am I enough?" is more about a person's own sense of inadequacy than any obstacle that might appear overwhelming. We all worry about our ability when entering any area with which we are unfamiliar. I recently had two conversations with friends who are considering new jobs. Both of these women would be great at the jobs they are applying for, but both were terrified of failure. Most people feel that way about starting to homeschool. Why? Like my friends and their new jobs, starting to homeschool is embarking on new territory. It is filled with risk, speculation and the unknown. It is messy and scary! We want guarantees. It is easier to believe that the public school will succeed in educating our children than it is to believe that we can succeed in educating our children at home.

OVERCOMING FEAR

I want to end Section 3 by discussing fear and sharing some ideas John Maxwell outlines in his book, *The 15 Invaluable Laws of Growth: Live Them and Reach Your Potential*. He addresses the issues of self-doubt really well. I just began reading it while writing this chapter and believe these ideas will sum up this section wonderfully, as he clearly outlines the fears that keep us from growing. He also identifies the gap between where a person is presently, versus where they want to be, and how to bridge it. He then covers the process of how to make the transition from fear to action.

I have followed Mr. Maxwell's outline, summarizing and expanding it to relate to homeschooling rather than personal growth, but the concepts are the same. These principles often hold us back from accomplishing things we're actually capable of, so it's important to understand and address them.

The Eight Growth Gap Traps

1. The Assumptions Gap

Here, Maxwell addresses the idea that we assume growth will happen automatically. He points out

 "No one improves by accident."[1]

In order to improve we have to make new choices, get training or practice the new skill. Everyone experiences tension when trying something new; that is part of the process.

The other side of the assumption gap is false perceptions. What assumptions are you making about the reasons you can't homeschool that aren't true? Or what are the assumptions you are making about what public school will provide your children that it won't? Align the truth with what action it will take to begin the steps needed to take you where you want to be.

2. The Knowledge Gap—"I Don't Know How to Grow"

Many people I talk to say something like, "I want to homeschool but there is so much I don't know; I don't know how to teach... I don't know what the best ...(method, curriculum, co-op, tools, etc.) are." It feels like a chasm from where they are standing to where they want to be, and they don't know where to start. Maxwell quotes Loretta Staples,

 "If you are clear about what you want, the world responds with clarity."[2]

Or as my dad always said, "Get moving and the things you are looking for will find you." There is so much information available today, experienced parents, online forums, conferences, and so on. Once you start pursuing information you will be surprised how many helpful people and resources you will find. I've listed a few books and sites in Appendix V. We've also recently launched a subscription-based resource at www.them.company. (**THEM** is a community of home educators dedicated to helping one another raise tomorrow's leaders, today.)

Ultimately, however, the knowledge gap will only be overcome as you begin to walk out the process.

3. The Timing Gap—"It's Not the Right Time to Begin"

What are you waiting for? Until it is easy? Until you can afford it? Until you feel confident? Honestly, if I waited for the right timing, I would still be waiting to homeschool! There is no perfect time.

Personally, I have also felt the other way. Fear that the moment or opportunity has passed. But all we have is today. So begin now. Take small steps if that is more comfortable. Maxwell quotes Leo Buscaglia,

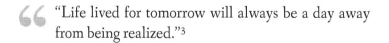

> "Life lived for tomorrow will always be a day away from being realized."[3]

4. The Mistake Gap—"I'm Afraid of Making Mistakes"

Don't worry, you will make mistakes, and often. Some of my best learning has come from making mistakes. Actually, one of my favorite stories to illustrate this point is from the invention of one of the five top-selling office products in the United States. It was a mistake, or at least not what the inventor intended it to be. Scientist Spencer Silver was trying to make a stronger adhesive but instead of his invention being super strong, it was super weak!

 "It stuck to objects, but could easily be lifted off. No one knew what to do with the stuff!"[4]

Four years later Scientist Arthur Fry was trying to put paper markers in his hymnal to keep his place but they kept falling out. He remembered his colleague Silver's weak adhesive he had invented years earlier at 3M. Fry coated his hymnal paper markers with the weak adhesive. They stayed in place and lifted off the page without damaging the book. Ten years after the original failure 3M began distributing Post-it® notes!

(An interesting fact - "In 1977, test-markets failed to show consumer interest. However in 1980, 3M implemented a massive consumer sampling strategy, and the Post-it® note took off."[5])

When we are so afraid of failure and mistakes, fear keeps us from trying. By trying we might fail, but we also might find a path we would not find any other way! Mistakes are part of success. Playing it safe just means nothing is going to change. Robert H. Schuller said, "What would you attempt to do if you knew you wouldn't fail?"[6] "Warren Bennis asserts, "A mistake is simply another way of doing things."[7] Mistakes are a part of learning and growing and as I said and have experienced, "there is grace for your process."

5. The Perfection Gap—"I Have to Find the Best Way Before I Start"

People are always in search of 'the perfect'; perfect car, perfect neighborhood, perfect diet, perfect job... When it comes to homeschooling, expectations are no different. One of the first questions parents tend to ask is, "What is the best science, math, spelling etc. curriculum, program, method...(you fill it in the blank). The assumption is there is a perfect way to do things, and with that perfect way, no pain. I love the quote for the beginning of the next section, "Le mieux est l'ennemi du bein (The perfect is the enemy of the good.)"[8] It is such a good motto to keep in mind when struggling with expectations. We may have perfect moments, but mostly we live in the good (or in the messy!). Complete perfection does not exist this side of Heaven. We may aim for it but we can't live there, not yet. But through the messy, we live a wonderful life. CS Lewis says it this way, "Aim at Heaven and you will get earth thrown in..."[9]

6. The Inspiration Gap—"I Don't Feel Like Doing It"

This is for the mom who needs help continuing homeschooling. That is why vision is so important. Know why you are doing what you are doing and be faithful. Try to be consistent, regardless if your toddler is wreaking havoc, if breakfast spilled on your math worksheet or if you've lost your cool. Regroup, apologize and keep going.

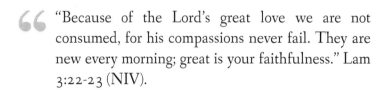

> "Because of the Lord's great love we are not consumed, for his compassions never fail. They are new every morning; great is your faithfulness." Lam 3:22-23 (NIV).

Jerome Bruner says, "You're more likely to act yourself into feeling than feel yourself into action."[10]

The same goes for your children. If they are having a hard time learning a concept, break it down. On days when math seemed overwhelming to my children, I would set a timer for ten minutes. I would say, "See if you can do five problems before the timer goes off?" Then I would praise their effort and say, "Wow. Now see if you can do six problems this time!" "Okay, now see if you can finish it before the next timer goes off!" "Hooray! You get a break!"

Sometimes the first ten minutes was all they could manage, and they needed the reward right then. That was okay with me because we broke the "I don't feel like doing it" barrier and made progress. The point is, life is made up of lots of small steps, many of which are undesirable. So it's important to learn how to tackle those, even when we don't feel like it. If we do that, the gift comes when we look back and see how far all those small steps have taken us!

7. The Comparison Gap—"Others Are Better Than I Am"

May I just confess that this is the one I struggle with the most! I have to keep my eyes on the Lord and not compare myself, my children, my house or my life against others! That is the wrong standard. The right standard is God and His Word. I know this intellectually, but I have to constantly remind my heart that it is the truth. Plus, just like people point out that Facebook is like a highlight reel, what we perceive about other people's lives is usually only bits and pieces. We tend to focus on the elements others seem to have success in that we don't. When we do that we can miss the areas where we are having success and maybe others aren't. The take away is not to focus on who is having success and who isn't, but to understand our paths are unique. Keep your eyes on the goal, humble yourself before God and keep moving forward. It is Him we are supposed to be concerned about pleasing.

8. The Expectation Gap—"I Thought It Would be Easier Than This!"

"You can't change your destiny overnight, but you can change your direction overnight." [11] Homeschooling, like anything of value, is hard. Don't let anyone tell you otherwise. There will be plenty of days you will want to quit. There will be seasons when you question if it's worth it. Again, that is why knowing what you are doing and why you are doing it are so important. You have to keep in mind that everyone who accomplishes something worthwhile did so through struggle.

Recently, we had a table-decorating contest for our church's Christmas luncheon. I was setting up our family's table. My friend's husband had arrived before his wife and two daughters so I asked where they were. He said, "They are on their way. They were up for hours last night working on their table design and couldn't agree on anything! It was so late, I finally said, enough of this and went to bed. They left early this morning to finish buying items for the table." As you might imagine, their table won the top prize for the most creative table.

Now a person might say they don't want to win if it means having to commit all that time and work and deal with the contention. But the cost to that attitude is, you may never win. My friend and her daughters pushed through, learned to give and take, grew together and in the end created something beautiful!

My favorite quote on this subject is from the movie *A League of Their Own*, which comes from a conversation between the main character Dottie Hinson (Geena Davis) and her baseball coach Jimmy Dugan (Tom Hanks). Dugan asks Dottie why she wants to quit playing baseball. She answers, "Because it got hard!" Dugan replies,

> "It's the hard that makes it good. If it were easy everyone would do it."[12]

Homeschooling is hard, it will take perseverance, commitment and determination, but like anything of value it is worth it.

Finally, in Maxwell's last section of the chapter he addresses some personal growth challenges in a sections called "Making the Transition to Intentional Growth:

1. Ask the Big Question Now
2. Do it Now
3. Face the Fear Factor
4. Change from Accidental to Intentional Growth"[13]

These statements can help us further clarify our concerns, define our goals and better understand the importance of taking action today as opposed to waiting until some future time.

Facing Your Fear

When I talk with parents they will often express fear associated with a particular subject or project like, doing a science fair experiment or teaching upper level math. Others are worried about the potential of teenage rebellion. (Usually, the parent has many years before they will face that situation.) If that is you and you are challenged with these fears, pray about them and prepare as much as you can, and then humbly continue. God will give you the grace when the time comes and He has answers you can't even imagine right now.

I remember hearing a story about a mom who was terrified about her son preparing for the science fair. The time finally came and she was overwhelmed with fear of facing the task. But as they began the process she was pleasantly surprised. First, her son was motivated and excited about the project so she didn't have to carry the whole burden like she had feared. Instead, she found her role was more about encouraging him and helping him organize and think through the process, areas she was good at and actually enjoyed contributing. There was a part of the experiment when they got stuck and went to the store to get more materials for the project. It just so happened that while they were in the store another customer overheard them talking about their project and he was extremely knowledgeable about that topic. He ended up spending about half an hour with her son, answering questions and sharing in her son's excitement. She couldn't have orchestrated a better learning experience for him if she had tried. In the end the science fair project became the highlight of their year.[14]

I could tell you story after story like this where, when the time came, the Lord was faithful. We are often fearful of the unknown, and the thought of making mistakes can be nearly paralyzing. But, in reality, the only way to succeed at times is to jump in and risk, and be committed to learning as we go. The beauty of homeschooling is that we aren't jumping in blindly, and we aren't jumping in alone. God has answers we may not be able to see immediately, but He is faithful to provide everything we need when we need it.

Intentional Growth

It's important to be as intentional as possible throughout the learning process. Intentionality is the structure that helps minimize mistakes and gives us a framework for addressing the ones we do make. For example, I joined an international homeschool group, Classical Conversations, and taught a weekly class to a group of eighth graders. One of the subjects I was the lead learner for was Latin. When I say lead learner, I literally mean *the lead learner* because I didn't know Latin at all! (Seriously, I was my typical one-week-ahead-of-the-students in learning.) I had experience in attempting to learn French and German—notice I said, attempting. By this time, however, I understood that the key to learning a second language is to have a solid grasp of the vocabulary and grammar rules of your first. My English grammar skills were terrible, so I was intentional about developing them, and, while learning Latin, to memorize its vocabulary and rules. So I found as many helps and support as I could and jumped right in.

In hindsight, I feel somewhat sorry for my first class of Latin students. I did my best, but today, six years later, I am very much aware of how weak my Latin was at that time. But the good news is, they all went on the following year with another Latin lead learner who was farther along in her Latin learning, and they did just fine. But here is the point: If I hadn't jumped in they would have had no Latin that first year, and I would not have begun the process of learning it either.

I made many mistakes along the way, but in the end we all grew. Since I was intentional about what I wanted to grow in, and what I wanted my children to grow in, we learned the foundation of Latin that year, which they built upon the following year. Through the process, the children (and I) not only learned some Latin, but we also learned about confronting the unknown and overcoming it, which is probably the more important lesson.

Final Thoughts

It is a big undertaking to shoulder the lead in your children's education. We all have fears and limitations, so it is natural to question the process and our ability. It's also common to perceive that it is easier for others. But the truth is, those who accomplish great things are not always the brightest and most gifted; rather, they are the ones who risk, adjust and humbly attempt the impossible -- and stick with it when it gets hard. Many, many parents started out with numerous questions and fears just like you and me and have homeschooled their children successfully. You can too!

∼

Section 3

LET'S GET REAL

What does successful homeschooling look like?

"Le mieuz est l'ennemi du bien."
(Perfect is the enemy of good.)

Voltaire, Philosophical Dictionary

9

LET'S GET REAL

I wish I could say that if you were to peek into my home this would be a typical homeschooling day...

It's 7:00 AM. I am in bed and my three children enter the room with a breakfast tray of freshly-baked bread, homemade jam, mouth-watering fruit and steaming hot coffee (one sugar, two creams). And with angelic voices in perfect unison they proclaim, "Blessed mother, we have all showered, cleaned our rooms, read our Bible and finished our math, which, thanks to you, is five grade levels ahead of our ages - may you live forever. We just wanted to check in with you before beginning our chores." I would sit up, and, with my skin radiant from a full eight hours of sleep and hair falling perfectly across my shoulders, respond with calm, serene tone, "Oh dear children, thank you! A thousand times, thank you. Yes, please do begin your chores, and then do the next couple of subjects. When you have finished, we will enjoy a delightful picnic lunch in the park...."

Obviously, I'm being facetious. But sometimes I get the impression that people think homeschooling is just like that!

Meanwhile, let me open the shades to the reality of a typical day...

It's 7:00 am and, if I'm cognitive, I am already thinking about going back to bed! The house is frightening. I look frightening. If we even get to breakfast it's a good day. When the children were younger they were usually up before I wanted to be. But as they became teenagers, waking them up and getting them out of bed could take up the first hour. Chores were hit or miss, even though we had a schedule chart with rewards and consequences. Schoolwork was generally accomplished, but many days with tears, some days with screams, others with complete tantrum meltdowns... and, from time to time, the kids had bad days too.

The truth is, homeschooling is real life. Siblings get along and they don't get along. They do some subjects well and struggle in others. They have loving attitudes and disrespectful attitudes. At times they comply wonderfully, and other times they don't. We had days where all schoolwork got done, and days where they *said* they got all their work done. We had days they out and out did not get their work done and didn't even try to hide it. I had good days when we accomplished wonderful things and I was really proud, and I had bad days of which I was ashamed. The secret to our success was, we got up every day and praised God, "His mercies are new every morning." Then we tried again.

One thing that has served us well is that we aim for the ideal, but we live in the real; and we don't beat ourselves up over it when the two do not align. When things go awry we assess, correct, apologize, forgive and keep going. Life happens: financial problems, relational issues, health problems, job changes...and so on.

They are all part of the journey.

In this section, I want to share some struggles we have had in hopes that it might help you avoid them, or to persevere if you face similar challenges. But I mostly want to look at this because, as Voltaire's "perfect is the enemy of good" rightly observes, it is important to distinguish the difference between perfect and good. Making this distinction helps us set realistic expectations so we recognize when what we are doing is indeed, good. If we don't understand what our expectations should be and are aiming for some perceived idea that isn't reality, we will be frustrated, and in time, we will burn out and everyone will lose. I don't want that to happen to you.

Aim for the Ideal, Live in the Real

I am not a perfectionist, but I struggle with idealism. Perfectionist: "a person who refuses to accept any standard short of perfection"; Idealist: "a person guided more by ideals than practical considerations."[1] I fall under the category of idealism and can therefore get discouraged if I don't accomplish what I hope for. Let me explain.

As I have mentioned, I have been a part of Classical Conversations for a number of years. One year I taught Challenge A (basically seventh grade). The students spend a whole year learning to draw a map of the world. They learn all the countries and capitals, along with the terrain features, and then draw everything from memory at the end of the year. I loved the idea, and Pierz and I worked on it faithfully. But at the end of the year, I was really disappointed because I had not done as good a job of ensuring he learned certain features such as mountain ranges, rivers, etc. as I had hoped. I felt like we had failed. We had spent the whole year of social studies on this project and I was upset and frustrated that I hadn't pushed him harder, and as a result he hadn't learned it as fully as we had set out to. I was dissatisfied and wallowing in some self-pity...until I pulled out the assignment he did at the beginning of the year on the first day of that class.

On that day the students were asked to draw the world from memory before we began the study. Pierz and most of the other students in the class drew seven circles on the page that first day. (Or should I say seven blobs!) When I compared that to the map he drew at the end of the year, the difference was incredible! Pierz, being an artist, took great care in the shapes of the actual continents and their placement on the grid. He knew most all the countries and capitals, all the oceans and even a few features. I realized that, though we hadn't reached the goal I had envisioned, our time spent wasn't at all in vain. He had learned a *tremendous* amount about geography that year. Instead of crying over what we missed, I needed to rejoice over what we accomplished. But my idealism kept me from seeing that at first. Throughout our homeschool life, I had to adjust my ideal to the real; and when I did, I was able to celebrate! Drawing a map of the world was one of those times.

We have to remember our children are people, not robots. They each learn at a different pace, have different strengths and weaknesses, and, importantly, they are in process. Education is more about them growing and developing than it is about us checking off boxes. It is wonderful if your child is the super-learner, exceptional-achiever, but that is not always the case. Often our children's performance may be average and even below average, and that is okay. They are in school for twelve years for a reason. It takes time to learn all the skills and to develop a solid knowledge base for adulthood. Much of life is about the process, not the destination. Again, only as I was able to put that in perspective was I able to rejoice.

Now, the positive side of idealism is that we aimed for the ultimate. In the map of the world example, we aimed for the ultimate by setting our goal on drawing the whole world, labeling the countries, capitals and features from memory and then worked diligently towards it. Had I at the beginning given an excuse for why that was too hard or unachievable for Pierz, I would have challenged him even less and limited our outcome even further. The goal was not unrealistic. The challenge was actually motivating, helping us aim for the ideal throughout the whole process.

I believe that is so important. The Bible says in Ps. 29:18 (NASB) "Where there is no vision, the people are unrestrained." Vision keeps us tethered to the goal. Vision, helps us stay focused, motivated and directed. It also keeps us disciplined and within necessary boundaries. We are tempted during the process to throw in the towel. Learning to keep the goal in mind and not letting yourself lose hope when the road is much harder than you ever imagined is crucial. Learning to accept your best when it is not exactly what you hoped for is also part of success. It's a delicate but necessary balance between the two.

10

THE HOW TO'S

I n this chapter and the next I am going to address questions parents often ask about the "How To's" of homeschooling. As mentioned, people are generally looking for "the best." What is the best math curriculum? Which is the best co-op? What is the best time to homeschool? What is the best way to organize the schedule? What is the best way to... fill in the blank. I understand what the parent is hoping for. But I want to suggest that this is not the right question, because it's not the right objective. A better question is, "What is the goal?" As we pointed out in the "perfect trap" there is no universal best or perfect curriculum, co-op, etc. Rather, there are numerous possible ways to successfully reach the goal. Finally, each family must consider their unique circumstances and work them into the equation.

This chapter will suggest some variables in such areas as schedules, mom's and dad's roles, working parents and single parents. I will share some thoughts on how homeschooling might look different depending on any one or a combination of these or other variables and how the goal of effectively homeschooling your children can still be accomplished.

Schedule

Scheduling is a great example of a variable with multiple effective options. Typically, most states require four hours of instruction a day for 180 days in grades 1-8, compared to the seven hour days of the government schools. (Homeschooling kindergarten is usually about two hours.) High School is different in that you are now concerned with credits. In Maryland, a credit for gym class requires 120 hours, whereas a math credit is more concerned with content covered than how long it may take to complete it. Since education regulations differ, check the requirements for your area.

This is important for understanding what is required for graduation as well. But most homeschoolers find they are able to accomplish their school work more quickly than in the typical public school day because of the time saved by the logistics of fewer students and the freedom to adjust to the individual. I am going to share some schedule styles (which are by no means the only styles) of real friends I know. Many have graduated their children and their children are successful adults!

Structured Friend's Schedule

I have a friend who has five children. Her homeschool day reflects the traditional school day schedule. Her children get up around 7:00 AM, get dressed, straighten their rooms and eat breakfast. She rings a bell at 8:30 AM and their school day begins. They have a schedule they follow where each subject, snack and activity has been given a specific time.

They are all in one room and she flows from child to child. The younger children generally do not use the whole time for a subject.

- 8:30-9:00 Bible
- 9:00-10:00 Math
- Snack
- 10:00-12:00 Language Arts (This includes reading, spelling, writing/cursive)
- 12:00-1:00 Lunch
- 1:00-2:00 Science/Social Studies (rotate weekly: two days one subject and three days other)
- 2:00-2:30 Other

These next three schedules are from the book, *Classical Christian Education Made Approachable*. I am an acquaintance of all three moms. You will notice "memory work" as part of their day. That is because these three families are all classical educators and memory work is an important part of classical instruction.

The Bortins Home

- 7:00-8:00 Bedroom & Breakfast – get up, clean room, eat, shower, walk/feed dog
- 8:00-8:30 Bible Study – We read the Scriptures so that we get our most important discussions completed for the day.
- 8:30-9:30 Math – We all sit at the same table and work, so I can answer questions as needed.
- 9:30-10:30 Language Arts
- 10:30-11:00 Memory Work
- 11:00-12:00 Science & Free Reading
- 12:00-1:00 Lunch & Recess

Over the years, I discovered that it was best to divide our day into four, one-hour academic periods. I'd spend 20 minutes of each period working with the youngest child, and then dismiss them to play. The older children have been trained to work independently during that time by looking at past lessons to see if they can solve a difficult math problem, etc.

The Courtney Home

- 8:00-8:30 Read Aloud
- 8:30-9:00 Story of the World (History)
- 9:00-9:30 Bible
- 9:30-10:00 Memorization & Recitation
- 10:00-11:00 Math
- 11:00-12:00 Language Arts
- 12:00-1:00 Lunch/Recess
- 1:00-1:30 Science & Free Reading
- 1:30+ Chores & Enrichment

The Shirley Home

- 7:00-8:00 Physical Fitness
- 8:00-9:00 Breakfast & Personal Devotions
- 9:00-10:00 Math
- 10:00-10:30 Independent Reading
- 10:30-11:00 Music Practice
- 11:00-11:30 Memory Work*
- 11:30-12:00 Writing, Editing & Presentation Work
- 12:00-1:00 Lunch
- 1:00-2:00 History, Science Reading & Research
- 2:00-6:00 More independent time for older students.

Activities during this time vary each day for each child.

- 6:15-7:00 Dinner Clean Up
- 7:00-7:45 Family Teaching & Discussion**
- 7:45-8:00 Poetry & Fables***
- 8:00-8:30 Family Devotions & Prayer***

* All memory work, with specific focus dependent on the day of the week

** All ages sit together and translate, present, or discuss a subject and integrate ideas. Focus again depends on the day of the week. This time is also used as needed for additional help with specific subjects.

*** Each family member takes a turn leading this reading and discussion.[1]

I appreciate and respect the organization of my four structured friend examples and wish I was more that way! Though I did have a schedule for each day, I must confess that I wasn't quite as consistent with the specific times for doing certain subjects. The important thing is figuring out what works best for you and your family.

Unstructured Friend's Schedule

On the flip side, I have another friend who has six children. They did not get up at any particular time, nor did they have any particular schedule. They did most subjects every day, but not always, and didn't stick to a specific order. Some days they got up at 9:00 AM, many days it was not until after 11:00 AM! They schooled at the table, on the front porch, in their rooms and in the family room. They were often still doing school at 5:00 PM.

Nocturnal Friend's Schedule

I have yet another friend whose husband worked at night cleaning office buildings. Often the whole family went and cleaned or hung out while the parents cleaned. This family did not start school till 3:00 PM in the afternoon many days and didn't finish until 8:00 or 9:00 PM. But neither did they go to bed until the early hours of the morning!

Again, it worked for them. One of the siblings has graduated from college and is doing exceptionally well in her career, and the rest are in college. I imagine they take later classes and study all night! But either way, they are wonderfully talented young adults and are all doing really well.

Classroom Friend's Schedule

I have other friends who have a designated school room in their home. It has white boards and tables or desks. There are cabinets with all the supplies labeled and organized. There are educational posters on the walls. All the school work is done in that room.

I always dreamed of having a homeschool room like that, but we didn't have the extra space.

Night Time Family-Friendly Schedule

I have a number of friends who school regular hours in their kitchen and living room, but clean up and put away all school-related materials before their husbands get home.

All Year Round, Summer Break and Combination Schedule

I have friends who do schoolwork all year round. They take breaks throughout the year, usually quarterly and coinciding with holidays. And I have friends who take traditional summer breaks, plus a few that do a mix of the two. Some do a couple subjects like math and or reading all year round, but the rest of their subjects they do only during the regular school year.

The Barry Home

Our family fell somewhere in between all these examples. While our days were more loosely structured, we found a flow that worked well for us.

From the beginning we were usually part of a co-op or some group that met once a week, so we structured our days on a four-day-a-week academic schedule. I also thought in terms of blocks of time and clustering subjects rather than each individual subject.

- 7:00 -8:00 Get up, make bed, get dressed, eat breakfast
- 9:00-9:30 Devotions (occasional chores which pushed back our start time for the next section)
- 9:20-11:50 Block One: Math, Reading, Writing, Spelling
- 12:00-12:30 Lunch
- 12:30-1:00 Sibling Time (could be playing outside, doing a fun craft or game together)
- 1:00-3:30 Block Two: Science, History, Health, Music or Art Classes

For me, addressing the core subjects of math and reading first thing helped me feel a sense of accomplishment. Otherwise, it felt like the weight of these subjects were hanging over my head until they were completed. The order of the subjects in Block One could change, but I was deliberate to ensure the core subjects were completed before lunch. The benefit in this was that it helped our afternoons be a little more relaxed.

Next, I always included some sibling time. I aimed for half an hour a day, but if they were having a great time and I felt it was productive, I would increase the time. I wanted my children to play and create and develop strong relationships with each other. Then when the neighborhood children came home, if they wanted to play with separate friends that was fine.

My goal was to end school between 3:00 to 3:30 PM. I didn't want school to drag on, as I also needed the time to just be mom, make dinner, make phone calls, go grocery shopping. Plus I worked a couple nights a week, so I wanted school done before I left. When the children were third grade and older, 3:30 was also homework time. That meant, if they had not done their work when they should have, it was homework and they had to complete it before going to play, or other activities such as dance lessons. It also meant it would be harder for them because I was not as available during that time. In other words, they knew they had me during the day. So, if they slacked off, they couldn't expect I was going to be as available later.

While I made sure each child received the help they needed, my goal was to help them to learn to take responsibility and to do what needed to be done during the allotted time. It is a delicate balance because they are learning these skills, so homework time looked different at nine years old versus 16 years old!

We took a traditional holiday and summer breaks because we all needed it, and summer was a fun time to do other activities we couldn't do during the year. Now, homeschooling does allow an added flexibility, so there were times we broke from our schedule.

We took trips during off seasons, we did special projects that required us to suspended our schedule for a while. Laurén was a dancer, and for many Christmases participated the Nutcracker Ballet. That meant from about three weeks at the end of November into early December our day consisted of afternoon and evening rehearsals. So I considered that and adjusted our workload before and after that season.

It is important to have goals and a plan because it actually allows you to be more flexible than when you don't have them. Having a plan lets you know where you can give in your schedule and where you need to tighten things up.

As the children got older, our schedule remained pretty much the same, in that we tried to complete the core subjects or whatever was most difficult first. But at this time I began training them to take more and more responsibility. When they were elementary age, I was the authority and in control. I would teach and guide all subjects and activities, and was very hands on.

As they got older their school work required more independent work. For example, their assignment might require reading a number of chapters, or writing an outline or first draft. I would help them create a schedule, including all their outside activities, and then help them be accountable as we worked. They would do a subject or two and then I would have them show me what they did. If they had questions or needed to process, I would help. If they hit a hard spot it would of course require more of my input. The goal was for them to grow in both responsibility and independence, while keeping in mind that they weren't ready to be fully either! Case in point, I had to check their work regularly, because their idea of done was not always in sync with what they had actually done!

As the children grew, the routine became easier because they were used to it and more mature. They still needed monitoring and guidance, but they knew the drill.

All of my friends mentioned in this chapter were successful homeschoolers, and their children turned out to be productive, well-adjusted adults whether they started school at 9 AM or 3 PM. The family's schedule may not have been consistent, but they were all consistent to faithfully and effectively school their children. The point is you can still be successful at homeschooling even if you think and operate beyond the public school structure, which is exciting!

Mom and Dad Roles

The roles of moms and dads (and grandparents) in homeschooling is just as diverse as the schedules and curriculum.

In our home, I did the majority of the hands-on schooling. Brett and I often discussed themes and strategies, with him fulfilling the role of principal (he operated very effectively at it, I might add) and leading most of the Bible and character training. I am a more permissive parent and Brett holds the absolutes better, so having him as the authority helped balance my sometimes free-spirited nature that the kids might otherwise take advantage of. Also, Brett worked from home for most of our homeschool years. This meant he was present, but the children knew his office had to be off limits during the day. It also meant we endeavored to be quieter than I would have normally required. But the children understood and adjusted.

I also have friends who co-teach. In one family the mother teaches four days while the dad works. The fifth day the dad stays home and teaches. And I know other families where the fathers stay home and educate the children and the mothers work full time.

I have also known families whose husband's don't participate much in the hands-on homeschooling at all. One of my friend's husband owns a number of successful companies and works late in the evening most nights. He has little to do with the teaching of the subjects, and, beyond that, he also asks respectfully that all schooling be finished before he comes home so he can enjoy his family. That doesn't mean the children don't share their learning with him, they do. But it means the mother predominately does the homeschooling.

I often hear moms complaining that their husbands aren't as involved with the homeschooling as they would like. But if your husband or wife is working full time, don't underestimate the contribution that he or she is making to your homeschool by being the provider—and thank them if you haven't lately. I am so thankful for the years of sacrifice Brett has contributed by working so that I could set my priority around the day-to-day involvement required to homeschool our children.

If your spouse's time is limited, and they want to be involved, they could read with the children at night or the children could share highlights of what they did during the day when they come home. You could also send photos or videos of the children's work and learning experiences to them wherever they are. This is a great way to stay connected throughout the week. In our area we have a homeschooling dads group that meets once a month to encourage the fathers in how they can be involved, which has been a great success.

The flexibility and diversity is part of the beauty of home-schooling. In your unique unit, you get to decide how the responsibilities are divided and what works for you. As long as the necessary bases are covered, the combinations of who does what are endless.

Working Moms and Dads

I have worked part time throughout most of our homeschool years. But my work has always been "jobs" over a career. My jobs usually didn't require much outside of my time at work and were flexible around my homeschool and family schedule. I have taught at various co-ops or at the YMCA where my children took classes. For quite a few years I was a waitress, and I loved it! I worked at night and I didn't feel like I was missing much because the children were in bed. Brett was able to be home most nights I worked, so I felt good knowing the children were in good hands, and it became a special time for the four of them.

Over the years, I have done a number of different jobs, but, again, I have always worked around the kids' and Brett's schedule. I enjoy working and making extra money, as well as the chance to get out and be with lots of people. (Did I mention I like to socialize?) I always came home rejuvenated.

But what about families where both parents work? Or what if you are a single parent? Is it possible to have a career and still homeschool? Surprisingly, there are parents that do both, work career jobs and homeschool; but their situation requires some unique considerations.

Laura Vanderkam, in her article, *How These Parents Work and Homeschool Too* notes there are 168 hours in a week. Then she quotes Pamela Price, author of How to Work and Homeschool.

> "Their school day and your work day do not have to mirror each other exactly. Work doesn't always happen from 9:00 AM to 5:00 PM Monday to Friday in an office (even a home office). And schooling need not happen these hours either. Once you wrap your head around that, the math makes sense. You can work 40 hours and homeschool for 20 hours, sleep eight hours a night (56 per week) and still have 52 hours for other things. The key is moving the pieces around."[2]

I agree that the schedule doesn't have to mirror the days and hours of government schools. Honestly, why we have school from September to June isn't really clear. Some suggest that school was set around the agrarian schedule for harvest; others say it was to accommodate families that would take a long vacation at a summer home or to compensate for "high absenteeism due to the hot and unhealthy summer months; epidemics, vacations and general truancy of students."[3] All we know is it became the norm.

So adjusting schooling to different time slots during the day or a different combination of days of the week are all acceptable.

On a practical note, Vanderkam remarks on the importance of some sort of child care for all working parents, even parents who work from home, and incorporating tutoring or co-ops in that care. I recently spoke with a single mom who is putting her children in a homeschool academy two days a week. Those will be her heavy work days. The other days she will be home with them and hire a babysitter for a couple of hours one of those days so that she can have focused work time. The babysitter is fluent in Spanish and will teach Spanish to the children as part of her responsibilities.

The working, homeschool parent requires a delicate balance of efficiency and organization. But as long as the child is truly being schooled and not just left to manage himself, I believe it is doable. One caution, there is a myth I hear often in homeschool circles that children educate themselves. It is true that in the high school years many students can be more self-directed, but even so, students always need the supervision, oversight and accountability of an adult. That is why we have teachers all through high school and professors in college. There are definitely the exceptions, students who are motivated and independent, but the majority are not. So that is why a co-op, tutor and sitter are helpful when your attention needs to be elsewhere.

I want to speak to the parent who desires to homeschool, but financially, emotionally or circumstantially, you just can't do that right now. I would suggest considering the hourly breakdown that Vanderkam points out. You could use some of the "52 hours" of free time to do some homeschooling even if your child attends a public school. Use a couple hours a week to do special books study, or take a field trip or do a project together. It will allow you to share in the education process with your child and connect with them in a special way. If it doesn't work out so that you can homeschool full time in the future, the accumulation of the few intentional hours a week over a number of years will still add tremendously to your child's education, as well as your relationship.

CURRICULUM

A s I said, when we started homeschooling there were just a handful of curriculum choices. Most approaches were pretty traditional and modeled the public school system. Today, however, there are many educational methods and philosophies. The mere number of curriculum choices is incredible, but this alone can leave a person feeling overwhelmed. If a family wants to homeschool, where do you even begin?

Since education in the U.S. is under the jurisdiction of each state, the process differs depending on which state you live in. Some states require you to submit a letter of intent, others do not. Other elements, such as whether you use an umbrella school or not, can affect your process.

We lived in Tennessee, so we registered under an umbrella school—an organization that helped manage our records. There is usually a fee for their services.

Our first step was to write a letter of intent to the school board letting them know we were going to homeschool. Then we signed up with the umbrella school and reported to them, initially sending a copy of the curriculums we intended to use. During the year we reported to them twice, once each semester, and showed our school work for that time frame. They kept a record of our attendance and grades. Many people don't use an umbrella school, working instead directly under their local school board and complying with their requirements. Some states have rather stringent rules and others are extremely lenient. I had no idea when we moved to Maryland that the rules from state to state could be so different.

If you are homeschooling in a country other than the United States, of course check with your country's rules. In a number of countries it is still illegal to homeschool. I am praying for that to change. But as our education becomes more global, there are options for international homeschoolers to gain accreditation through organizations outside their home country (e.g., www.NARHS.org). This is significant for homeschooling families, especially if it is legal in their country to homeschool but there is not provision for accreditation for them like we have under our public school boards in America. This way, international families do not risk their children's education being unaccredited.

So it is important to learn the standards of where you live and to make sure you are compliant. (In the USA go to - www.ed.gov, then search your state for its homeschool regulations.)

Once you have registered, the next step is to choose your curriculum and subject focus. I say subject focuses because depending on your methodology, you don't have to have books for every subject area or grade level like traditional school. For example, I often combined subjects like History and English. Say we were studying the Middle Ages. I would choose books and novels about topics that related, and we would study grammar and write about the history content, thereby covering our objectives for English.

Actually, the more you can integrate the elements your children are learning, the better. Public education currently teaches all subjects as individual topics and it is as though they should never meet. But, in reality, all learning integrates. Chemistry depends on a basic knowledge of algebra. Most subjects require reading, spelling and comprehension skills. The development of thought in science is heavily influenced by the events of history and vice versa.

I share this because often parents feel the pressure to have eight different subject curriculums to cover all the material that needs to be taught. Then they feel pressure to cover every suggestion, every question and every worksheet that comes with them. That is practically impossible and would take all day, all night *and* every weekend!

But if you consider the idea that the goal is to teach skills and equip our children with tools on how to learn, you realize the content is what we use to teach, not the other way around. So understand what your goals are first and use the curriculum to support the learning of the skills. The only exception is math. And, even then, while you should be diligent to cover all the concepts in a curriculum grade level, not every single problem needs to be completed (although there is certainly great benefit from getting all the practice).

Basic Guidelines When Choosing Curriculum

1. Have Goals and Skills in Mind

I have mentioned this before, but it merits repeating. Many people approach curriculum as the standard of measurement, when in fact the curriculum is more like the tool you use to get to the standard. For example, in first grade math your goal is to teach the basic skills of numbers (basic facts, adding and subtracting) and other foundational skills. So you look for a curriculum that teaches those skills. Since a large variety of curriculums will cover that material very well, you have the freedom to choose the one that you like best. I found for math with smaller children I liked a workbook with consumable pages. At one point when picking a second grade math book, I had gotten it down to a number of perfectly acceptable curriculum, but I chose one over the others because it included pictures of places around the world. The pictures had nothing to do with the math, but I liked taking about the different places and finding them on the globe each day.

As the children got older we moved to a more traditional textbook, which I could re-use with multiple students. Personally, I have never liked doing math solely on a computer. I wanted to be able to see the child's thought process when figuring out a problem, so writing it down helped. Plus, within the digital realm, the student can sometimes guess and skip the actual math, which defeats the purpose. But I know for some children online math programs are a great fit, especially if they have dysgraphia issues. I did use teaching DVD's in the upper levels of math and found them very helpful.

Again, that's why there are so many choices. And you get to choose what fits your teaching and your student's learning style. But the main take away is to know your goals and the skills you are trying to teach, and then choose curriculum that supports them and suits you.

2. Know Your Purpose

To us, establishing a Biblical worldview and developing critical thinking skills was very important. So we looked for curriculum that supported such process. With my third child, Pierz, he was naturally quite bright but needed help with character growth. I think for the first couple of years I picked books and curriculum almost completely on the criteria that they reinforced basic principles like honesty, integrity and long suffering because that was what he needed.

We also wanted our children to have strong communication skills and the option to go to college, so we chose programs that were solid academically.

3. Cost

Another important consideration is cost. What is your budget? Is the curriculum consumable? How many children do you have? Is it something you can use with multiple children? We were on a very tight budget for many years when we homeschooled so cost was a determining factor. Used curriculum sales are a great help and the library is a wonderful resource. Check online for used books (e.g., www.homeschoolclassifieds.com, or www.homeschoolbuyersco-op.org), the Goodwill and Wonder Book. Also check local homeschool groups, as they often host book sales. These are also helpful if you want to recycle your old books.

4. Method and Learning Styles

Method of education usually refers to the guiding philosophy of how students learn and should be taught. This is different than student learning styles, which considers how children receive information. The two concepts do slightly overlap, and some people consider learning styles a method of education. I have listed very brief descriptions of the main methods. I don't believe all the methods are apples to apples, but I have included them so that you will be familiar with the terms.

Methods include such approaches as:

1. Traditional – modern education model such as in typical schools today done at home.
2. Classical Model – Develops strong thinking and speaking skills, and teaches how to learn anything. Follows the natural stages of learning through the arts of learning grammar, dialectic and rhetoric.
3. Charlotte Mason – nourishes each child, uses narration, living books, nature study, art, play, real life situations.
4. Waldorf – emphasis is the whole child, encourages creativity, self-awareness, discourages computers and T.V.
5. Unit Study – learning a topic in-depth and the skills of traditional subjects are learned in the context of the overall topic.
6. Montessori – children learn at their own pace, children select own materials, believes children will be drawn to what they need.
7. Un-schooling – often child led, learn from their own interests, don't use curriculum.
8. Eclectic uses a combination of any or all methods above.

I have used a number of methods throughout the years but prefer the classical model because it is the most logical and effective approach to learning. This is because it best facilitates the natural progression of how we learn (input, processing, output) and the development of critical thinking and communication skills. I have included some wonderful books and website references in Appendix V.

Learning Styles include:

- Auditory – learn through speaking and listening

- Kinesthetic – learn through tactile, hands on learning, manipulatives, etc.
- Visual – images, maps, pictorial representation
- Read and Write – learn through words, taking notes and reading

Being aware of different learning styles helps when it comes to figuring out how your child best memorizes, organizes and retrieves information. Part of being a successful learner is knowing how you best acquire and retain information. On the flip side, I would caution a parent from becoming too focused on their student's particular learning style and not teaching them to grow and adapt by using the other styles too. In life, the world rarely adjusts to our needs. Rather we need to be able to adjust and adapt to navigate it well. Personally, I am an auditory learner. A lot of learning requires reading, which I can do, but I much prefer to listen. So whenever possible, I get an audio book. But if that isn't an option, I have also developed my reading skills so that I can still accomplish the needed learning.

Finally, incorporating multiple learning styles helps children become more well-rounded students.

5. Teacher Friendly

I liked curricula that were pretty straightforward and easy to follow. I have friends who preferred versions that told the parent almost word for word what to say. I didn't need that but I respected those who wanted that extra support. You will be using the material, so make sure it makes sense to you and that you can follow it. Some curricula is teacher-directed, and some is more student-directed. Be aware of your time constraints and your child's needs. If it requires more time to prepare than you have to give, you won't do it. Likewise most children need direction and accountability. Try to find the balance that works for you both.

6. Get a Basic One and Build Creatively From There

I am a creative, visionary type of person, so it was important to me to do fun, outside the box projects with my children that we would all enjoy. As such, I decided one year to create original approaches for all of their subjects. It was a very inspiring plan, prompting many wonderful ideas! What I quickly found out, however, was that with three small children, car repairs, doctor and dentist appointments, keeping my marriage a priority, working part-time, and on and on, being creative all the time was more of a hit or miss proposition (mostly miss!). That meant we had days when I didn't have time to create anything; it also means I had no back up! Ugh. So, I quickly learned the value of having a stable, basic curriculum as a foundation. That way when inspiration hit, I could easily take the lesson to a more creative, imaginative level. But when I was just trying to get through the day, I had a solid program to work from.

7. Check It Out, Read Reviews and Talk to Other Parents

Now that homeschooling is considerably more popular, there is a wealth of information available regarding curriculum strengths and weaknesses. Check out sites like, www.homeschoolreviews.com. Go to homeschool conventions and used curriculum sales, talk to other people who have used the curriculum you are interested in and, whenever possible, personally review the actual curriculum before purchasing it. Most states have homeschool conventions or curriculum fairs where many book vendors attend and display their products. Our organization is www.machemd.org, which stands for The Maryland Association of Christian Home Educators.

8. Changing Curriculum

If you buy something and hate it, you can stop using it and get something else. You have that freedom. But just a heads up, sometimes the greater challenges are not in the curriculum itself. For example, I was talking to a parent the other day who was frustrated with the math curriculum she was using and wanted to switch to another one. After spending some time talking to her it became obvious that her son was struggling with math and study skills in general. A different book wasn't the answer. She had to slow down and repeat some concepts and give him more time to learn them.

In other cases, the challenge is a weakness of the parent. I wanted to teach my children Latin. I'm pretty sure I tried nearly every curriculum on the planet...for about two weeks...and then quit. I couldn't find one I liked! I eventually discovered that the problem was not the curriculum, it was me. The truth is, I didn't understand the importance of grammar structure in teaching a language. Once I was able to pinpoint and address my area of weakness, we were able to stick with a Latin curriculum. I am happy to report that after that we improved in both our English and Latin learning! (And today, I'm using those principles to learn Greek.)

9. Practical Approach to Breaking Down a Curriculum

One organizational tool that worked well for me, and helped us complete a curriculum within the year, was to break it down into sections so I had check points that allowed me to ensure we were on track.

Here are the steps I would take:

- First, I would divide the subject in half, meaning I would set the goal of being on a certain page/section by the end of January.
- Next, I would further divide it into monthly sections.
- Then each month's section into four weeks.
- Finally, I'd divide each week into four days (because of our weekly co-op class).

So, for example, if a math curriculum had 120 lessons, my goal was 60 lesson completed by the end of January. Next I would divide those halves into five sections each, so I would have a goal for each month. For example:

- September = Lessons 1-20.
- October = Lessons 21-40, and so on.

Then I would divide each month into weeks:

- Week One = Lessons 1-5.
- Week Two = Lessons 6-10, etc.

If we were going on a field trip or had a dentist appointment or something and I knew we would miss a day, I would double up and do extra pages/concepts on another day. This way I had a daily goal, a weekly goal, a monthly goal, as well as a halfway mark, each providing check points to help us stay on schedule throughout the year. It was really helpful since I could then know at a glance whether we were pacing well or needed to adjust. It also helped me compensate for the unexpected.

As time went on, I found December was usually a weak month for us school-wise because of the holidays, whereas

January and February were good months because we were usually stuck at home due to inclement weather. I would take that into account during my planning and add a few extra lessons to the fall to help compensate for December. I also worked hard in January and February so that when spring came we could ease up a little and enjoy the weather and still finish well by the beginning of summer.

This worked for us, but a lot of parents I talk to today express being tired and burned out in January and February. So if that is you, slow down during those times. The goal is to pace yourself and your family by developing a stride that serves your learning process.

10. Using It All

Don't be a slave to the curriculum. As mentioned earlier, you may not use all of the material or use it all the way they suggest. That is fine. Remember, the curriculum is the tool that supports the learning, not the other way around. Keep your eye on the skills and the goals like we talked about at the beginning of this chapter.

∾

WHAT TO EXPECT WHEN YOU HOMESCHOOL

I'd like to share a few thoughts about how children learn at different ages and stages, and how that might affect your homeschooling process. It is a different world when your children are all in their preschool or elementary years versus their teens, or, for that matter, when they're spread across the age spectrum.

My purpose in adding this section is to create a starting point for you in your understanding of how your child's physical and emotional development affects their learning and to help identify what are normal academic focuses and expectations during these stages. These sections address typical concerns and struggles many parents have expressed. My hope is that this chapter will assist you in setting realistic expectations as you manage each stage. We forget what it's like to be a seven year old who would rather play than do math, a twelve year old who feels caught between being a child and a teenager, or a fifteen year old who is more concerned with how they look than their future goals. But despite the struggles, each age and stage brings wonderful opportunities for important growth and learning.

I've provided here only a general overview because there is so much written on this topic, and in much greater detail than I could do justice.

PRESCHOOL: 3-5 Years Old

The physical growth and amount of cognitive learning between birth and school age in a child is amazing. Children learn to walk. They learn a language. They develop social skills and the foundations of their personalities. The parents are the primary teachers and most of this learning is accomplished through informal interaction.

Academic

Formal education starts in kindergarten, with younger children generally spending their early years at home or in a similar nurturing environment. But today the trend in education is moving more and more towards starting children earlier in a structured educational setting known as preschool. But where does the concept of preschool come from, and is it the best way to develop the readiness skills in children?

"Head Start, the first publicly funded preschool program, was created in 1965 by President Johnson. The federal government helped create this half-day program for preschool children from low-income families. Head Start began as a summer pilot program that included an education component, nutrition and health screenings for children, and support services for families... By 2005 sixty-nine percent, or over 800,000, four year-old children nationwide participated in some type of state preschool program."[1]

So academic preschool is a really new concept too, much newer than even government schools; yet most parents today consider it an important part of the education system. Part of the philosophy in the United States is that we believe 'the sooner the better.' We think, "What is better than a five year old reading?... A three year old reading!" But is it? There is considerable research that indicates the opposite.

For most children, the formal learning of reading and math are best left until the elementary years. Even so, parents of young children often feel pressure to start academics early in order to give their children a head start. Interestingly, however, and to the contrary, most experts believe that this stage in a child's life is for creating a foundation of experiences that helps them become ready to learn when they are school aged. I agree with Jenifer Wana's, author of *How to Choose the Best Preschool for Your Child,* experience with this, "Although parents may take comfort in knowing their child is in a more academic setting, some say this only makes a difference in the short term. 'A lot of people put children in Montessori, for example, because they want them to learn academics early. Research shows that's true only up to a certain point,' Jenifer Wana says. Preschool [age] is time to learn social and emotional skills so you are ready to learn those academic skills later on."[2]

Academic skills cover a very broad spectrum. I am not saying that it's wrong to teach your children to recognize letters, numbers, colors and shapes, etc., "God has designed young brains with a facility to memorize in order to prepare them for the next stages of learning. Toddlers learn to speak their native language by listening and memorizing sounds and words. Preschoolers learn to read by memorizing the alphabet and its associated sounds."[3]

 What I would caution parents about is the idea of pushing their children ahead in structured academic pursuits and thinking that the measure of their success is whether they are capable of performing "school type" behaviors at this stage.

This can be detrimental, causing children to be frustrated and stressed, which may delay academic skills later on. Instead, it is important to understand what skills should be the focus for a preschooler.

Readiness and Play

The goal for the preschool child is readiness. Readiness is a set of basic components that the next thing (kindergarten/first grade) can be built on. The basic components are skills such as putting on his own coat and going to the bathroom unassisted, holding a pencil or cutting with scissors and getting along with others. Even with the list of readiness skills, parents will find that children vary greatly in their ability in these areas at this age, and that is okay. These are the skills they are developing. The caution here is that the readiness skills educators are generally talking about when they refer to the preschool years are not being able to read, write, and do arithmetic. Again, however, these are not skills they must learn at this stage, and forcing them to do so can hinder their learning later.

So what is desired? How do children learn at this age? Through play!

 "Play enhances language development, social competence, creativity, imagination, and thinking skills... play is the chief vehicle for the development of imagination and intelligence, language, social skills, and perceptual-motor abilities in infants and young children."[4]

An example of how children learn the desired readiness skills through play is demonstrated by their typical interaction with playdough: "...children cooperate with peers, communicate their ideas through spoken language, express themselves through creativity and dramatic play, learn about the effects they can have on their environment, and experiment with scientific concepts. Experiences with playdough allow children to explore and experiment in various ways. Learning occurs in social, emotional, language, physical, and cognitive domains, helping to provide children a solid foundation for future schooling."[5] Wow, all that from playing with playdough.

Going to a park, playing outside, playing with blocks, dolls and other toys, helping mommy or daddy cook, clean, sweep, all this is appropriate and beneficial play for preschool children. Try not to be in a hurry with your children's formal education. These rich, natural experiences are providing a very important foundation, much more than we often realize.

Children benefit from playing with each other, playing by themselves, watching others play and by playing with their parents. "Parental involvement in a child's world of play is not only beneficial for the child but is extremely beneficial to the parent. Playing with children establishes and strengthens bonds that will last forever. Parent-child play opens doors for the sharing of values, increasing communication, allowing for teachable moments and assisting in problem solving. Playtime provides opportunities for the parent and child to confront and resolve individual differences, as well as family related concerns and issues. Finally, it allows the parent to view the world through the eyes of a child once again."[6] Isn't that quote encouraging! As chaotic as this stage of child rearing feels, remember they do grow fast. Although, sometimes it can feel like it isn't fast enough! I remember one friend saying she would be counting down the hours until bedtime, and then be dying because it wasn't even yet time for dinner!

I realize that sometimes parents simply need a break, so a preschool for a couple hours a week can be a great option. To help me keep my balance, I put Laurén in a Mother's Day Out program once a week when she was young. I used it less for Brooks, and by the time I had Pierz, it didn't really provide the break or benefit I was initially seeking. Experience and group dynamics has also impacted my philosophy. Managing three children, I found it easier to keep Pierz at home, and I felt the benefit of him being with his siblings and under my care far outweighed the advantages of the Mother's Day Out environment.

Incidentally, I just heard a testimony of the benefits of being at home with other siblings. The child, a two year old, was born prematurely at 29 weeks and had been in physical and speech therapy for the past year. Her therapist visited their home to conduct an in-depth review of the child's skills. At the end of her review the therapist reported that the child was above average and greatly attributed her rapid increase in scores to..."being surrounded by her older siblings all day." The therapist noted that she probably would not have grown so rapidly in a preschool surrounded by other two-year-olds. The mix of ages in a home is extremely beneficial for the development of all the siblings. The younger siblings benefit by exposure to the advanced language and the modeling of more mature social interaction of the older siblings. The older siblings benefit by teaching, leading, nurturing and considering the younger siblings.

Nurturing the Soul

Nurturing the soul of a preschooler is also really important. It has always intrigued me that Moses remained in his home until he was weaned, and was then transitioned to life in the palace.

During those early years, I imagine his mother Jochobed praying over him while she nursed him and sharing her knowledge and relationship with God. Those early years set the foundation for Moses' life of ministry and connection with the Lord. We can do the same with our little ones.

My main point with this section is to free you from the pressure of worrying about your child's future academic performance and thinking they need an outside scholastic environment such as a preschool at this age, or that you need to pressure them to preform "school like academics" in order to give them a learning edge. Again, there is a significant amount of literature warning that such pressured learning at the preschool stage can even be detrimental (see *The Hurried Child,* by David Elkind).

Secondly, this section is to help explain what an academic environment means for the preschool years and encourage you that you can easily provide all they need at home, and to remind you of the great value of interaction between you and your child and family as you engage in the natural activities normally associated with this age: reading lots of stories, going to the park, feeding the ducks, digging in the dirt, swinging on the swings, playing house...and playing with playdough. In the words of Mr. Rogers, from the beloved T.V show *Mr. Roger's Neighborhood,*

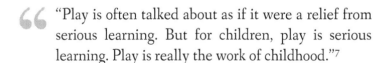

> "Play is often talked about as if it were a relief from serious learning. But for children, play is serious learning. Play is really the work of childhood."[7]

And it doesn't stop being important after age five. So don't feel the pressure to minimize this stage to traditional academics and a structured environment. Instead, relax and play!

Conclusion

Readiness and play are important building blocks for preschoolers. Hold your children close, read lots of books, interact with them, and help them interact with others. Remember, when you are feeling overwhelmed by the 24/7 supervision required for children at this age, that it is short lived, because they do grow fast. Really fast. So take courage. The time intensive preschool years are significant years. Many foundational skills are being learned through normal, everyday interaction.

ELEMENTARY: 5-12 Years Old

"From starting school to entering puberty, age five to 12 is a time of great progress and development for your child. While the changes may be more gradual, your child's thinking, emotions and body will continue to develop."[8] Academically we often divide these years into two categories: early elementary, grades 1-3 (often including kindergarten) and later elementary, grades 4-6. The main goal of the elementary stage is to teach a foundation of information and the fundamentals of reading, writing and arithmetic. So much of learning is accomplished through those basic skills that they are the focus for this phase.

"Between age six and ten, children are able to better understand and think about several elements of an issue. However, they are still likely to think in very concrete terms and only about things they can experience for themselves."[9]

Elementary children are developing all the building blocks for learning. If you were to compare it to a computer, this stage would be the input stage.

Academic

I agree with the classical model that recognizes and utilizes the natural ability of elementary aged children to memorize large amounts of material. Like the opening quote explains, children at this age tend to be concrete. They just want the facts. I bet by experience you know it's true. Have you ever had a five year old ask you where babies come from? I remember when my daughter asked me. We were at a park with some friends when she ran up and asked me the question. At first, I panicked because of the nature of the topic. How much do you share? Where do you start? I began with a simple statement like, "They come from a mommy's tummy." I was getting ready to say more and she said, "Oh!" and skipped off. That was enough information for her. I was about to answer the question from the perspective of an adult and had misread her needs as a child. Not that you can't share more, of course you can. Not that there aren't times they want more input, there are. But in general, they are not looking for more than a statement or some facts.

So take advantage of their natural curiosity and memorization skills by inputting as many facts, names, dates, events and basic vocabulary of subjects as possible!

 "There is a big push in modern educational theory to introduce abstract concepts to elementary children, and while there is some overlap of the stages with individual children maturing in their thinking individually, for the most part they are not developmentally able to grasp abstracts at this age... ideally, an understanding of anything is not the goal at this age, but rather: have they memorized their math facts and demonstrated that by being able to do computations; have they memorized their phonics and spelling rules and demonstrated that by being able to read and spell correctly; and so on. The problem with attempting to teach abstracts at this age is that children do not yet have the ability to connect relationships between factors, nor do they have the ability to question and reason out the validity of what they have been told, but they have the ability to believe that what they have been told is the truth."[10]

So spend these years laying the foundation of subjects and teaching the tools of learning.

What's Normal?

My first practicum of student teaching in college was with a veteran first grade teacher of almost 40 years who was retiring at the end of that school year. She said there was a correlation between reading readiness and physical development. This became clear through the observation of a rambunctious boy who showed no interest in reading. A few weeks into my practicum, however, he began to settle down and started to engage more in class activities, especially reading. We talked about it and she asked me if I noticed anything different about him that might have affected his change. Unfortunately, I didn't. Then she told me to look closely at him when he smiled. So I did. This time I noticed he had lost a tooth. She had me study all 20 children in the class and assess their teeth and how well they were doing with reading. Surprisingly, I did notice a correlation. She said that in many European countries educators believed children were not ready to read until they lost their first tooth, so they didn't even attempt teaching them to read until then.

Since then, through further study and experience, I believe

there is truth in her observation. We accept that children grow physically at different rates and understand that there is a wide range of what is considered normal. The same is true for a child's cognitive development. Children grow at different rates, thereby creating a pretty wide range for what falls in the normal category, and we need to keep that in mind. "Some children lose their first tooth as early as four or as late as seven."[11] Not surprisingly, children learn to read between the ages of four and seven, with the girls on average learning on the earlier side and boys on average learning on the later. And research supports that there is "no difference between the reading ability of early (from age five) and late (from age seven) readers by the time those children reach their last year at Primary School by age 11."[12]

One last helpful finding from the study quoted above is, "One theory for the finding that an earlier beginning does not lead to a later advantage is that the most important early factors for later reading achievement, for most children, are language and learning experiences that are gained without formal reading instruction,"[13] says Dr Suggate. "Because later starters at reading are still learning through play, language, and interactions with adults, their long-term learning is not disadvantaged. Instead, these activities prepare the soil well for later development of reading."[14]

I love the wisdom in the second part of the quote. The later starters are still learning important skills for reading even though they are not reading independently yet. The time is not being wasted, rather, it is vitally important. These findings support the value of the early learning strategies we discussed in the previous preschool section in relation to learning to read. At this stage you are formally teaching letters, sounds, etc., but being mindful that if your five, six or even seven year old isn't reading yet, that it doesn't mean they aren't learning and growing in reading skills. (Of course, there are learning disabilities and other factors that could affect delayed reading. And if you suspect something else affecting learning there is no harm in checking with specialists.) But the point is, if your child is struggling with reading and they are under seven years old it doesn't necessarily mean they have a learning disability.

Basic Study and Character Skills

Along with learning basic academic skills, you will find that other important basics such as character training and study skills are equally important. Study skills like sitting still, listening and following direction can take as much patience to teach as anything else. I remember a friend moaning about spending half the year of first grade working with her daughter to sit still for any length of time. Other parents struggle with getting their children to follow their directions, and not whine or fuss. These attitudes can wear on a parent and they feel like unnecessary distractions when you are trying to teach. But a large part of homeschooling (and learning in general) is dependent on establishing and maintaining discipline and respect. So don't be surprised if your children display attitudes. Remember that training the character is part of the development process.

As a teacher, classroom management is a significant part of successful teaching, and it is no different with homeschooling. I've had people say to me many times, "I could never do what you do. My child and I would kill each other!" The fallacy in that statement is the assumption that my children and I easily or seamlessly dealt with our natures. I wish that were true. The truth is, we had to learn how to overcome ourselves and push through despite our weaknesses.

To be fair, it is true that people have different temperaments, and some are easier to work with than others, so I don't want to dismiss the reality that character training challenges can differ from family to family and child to child. I have a friend who had two children that were very cooperative. She would hear her friends complain about fighting with their children to get dressed in the morning, and she would say, "Just make them put their clothes on, for heaven's sake! How hard can it be?" Then she had her third child...and had to repent!

She admitted, "I had no idea how stubborn and difficult a child could be! My first two were so compliant. But with my third, everything is a battle!"

As difficult as it was, my friend still had to figure a way to get pants on the child. Similarly, with our children, as willful or whiny as they may be, we have to address their character and personality issues that affect learning and, honestly, address ours too. Remember, it is a mistake to think that by sending them to school those character flaws are going to go away on their own. They will need to be addressed because, sooner or later, they will rear their ugly heads. I respect my friend who took that six months in first grade to help her daughter establish the skill of sitting still. She set a reasonable expectation; she didn't make her sit there for hours, but neither did she ignore the need for her daughter to grow in the skill. She worked with her diligently and patiently.

At the elementary age you will have to set patterns and boundaries for your children, understanding that each one may struggle with different character and or learning aspects. It's hard when other people don't seem to have to work with their children like you do. But every home has its issues, and Scripture wisely instructs us not to compare. God gave you your children to work His purpose in them and in you! I wish I could say that we successfully worked out all our children's character flaws, or our own. But we didn't. But many were addressed, and we did all grow.

The elementary years are extremely valuable for laying the

foundational skills that the rest of learning is built on. So don't underestimate the importance of taking the necessary time to teach academic basics (reading and math skills), beginning study habits (sitting still, following instructions) and character development (respect, humility). Be faithful to work on these skills for as long as it takes for your individual family. In the big picture, it is a very small investment; but the return is tremendous.

Nurturing the Soul

The final point I would like to make about teaching elementary age children is regarding the unique window of opportunity it holds for you to be the dominant voice in your child's life. They want to be told answers, and they will receive your input almost without question.

When I speak to parents to help illustrate their influence I like to tease that during this stage of parenting I was like the queen of the castle. If I went to the grocery store alone (a miracle in itself!), my return was treated like a royal entrance. The hugs, the kisses, "I missed you!" would do any ego good. Your children are the same with you. They love you and want to please you. You are the center of their world.

I recently watched a Facebook video that beautifully illustrated this point. It asked parents if they could pick anyone to have a dinner with, who it would be? Then they showed the parents the video of their children (elementary aged) being asked the same question. The parents choose famous people. Without fail, the children chose to have the dinner with their parents. As the parents realized how influential they were to their children, many cried. It was extremely touching to witness.

During the elementary years parents have tremendous impact in their child's life, even though the process can be totally exhausting at times! But I hope to help you understand that these years provide a window for significant, foundational influence that may not be guaranteed later. So it is extremely important that you are deliberate and strategic during this stretch by teaching Bible verses, facts, and the principles based on absolute truth. When they look to you for answers and support, give it realizing that your time and energy are making a lasting impact. You are tenderly nurturing them to grow in confidence so they can make sense of this world and understand their unique contribution to it. This is accomplished by the stability and safety your children receive from your consistent care, and it is what they will begin to test and build upon in the next stage.

Conclusion

The elementary years are a wonderful season in the parenting journey. The combination of your child's personal growth and deep love for you makes these years a great opportunity for laying the foundational skills both academically and as individuals. During this time they will grow in character and learn the basic skills of reading, writing and math upon which all learning is built.

MIDDLE SCHOOL: 12-14 Years Old

During the ages of 12-14 years old, "normal" can cover a very broad spectrum. In my mind's eye I can still see my youngest son, Pierz, standing with a group of his friends when he was twelve years old. Most of the girls towered over him, and half the guys looked like men while the other half like boys; yet they were all about the same age! Not only do their bodies begin to go through puberty, mentally and emotionally they change as well. One day they want to be treated like an adult and the next day they want to be your little one again. They can be moody, argumentative, and vacillate between being overly confident and overly insecure. As our children grow and develop so do their thinking skills; they no longer want to just be told the answers, they want to process and begin to come to their own conclusions. Despite their growing independence, your influence and leadership are still extremely important.

Academic

Up until this point, most learning has been concrete concepts, recall and lighter processing, which do not typically require a great deal of formal studying. But as school progresses, study skills (how to organize, recall and express information) become more necessary. The amount of material expands and answers are often comprised of multiple parts. A key study skill is the ability to write down the steps in a process. The working through of the parts and doing it step by step is important in training the mind to critically analyze information. Teaching skills such as, taking notes, writing chapter summaries, creating outlines and making flash cards are important tools. I'll use a math example to demonstrate this principle.

You will have students who don't want to show their work in algebra. Until this point, most arithmetic has not required multiple operations to get the answer because they have been learning the basic operations. Since a question only required one or two steps, students may have been able to do the majority of the work without showing their steps for getting the answer. They may still be able to do a lot of the work in their head at first. But getting the answer is not the only skill math teaches. Being able to demonstrate the process and steps is equally important to getting the correct answer. Here are just three of the many reasons why it's valuable to write down the process. First, if the student makes a mistake the area of confusion can be more easily identified. Secondly, the mental exercise of breaking the problem down trains them to problem solve with precision and accuracy, skills that transition beyond math. And finally, like all math, algebra builds upon itself. If the student hasn't intentionally broken down the process throughout the foundational stages, they will become lost in the advanced stages.

Detailed processing is a new skill at this age and therefore requires hard work. Because of this, don't be surprised if you get push-back. If they are resistant, it's important to identify whether it's a character flaw or a learning challenge. Additionally, some students take longer to master the systematic thinking of problem solving, so they need a lot of practice. Work diligently with your student and consider their progress compared to their previous work, not compared to the work of others.

At this age, your student will begin growing towards taking responsibility for their learning. In middle school, I could explain the lesson to my children and they could do a lot of the practice on their own. So if it was History, they could read the section and answer the questions, or I could assign them a step in the process of writing a paper and they could go work on that. Even so, I still had to monitor and engage with them often. If I had just given them a list of everything to do, it would have never gotten done.

On a practical note, have your children keep their study materials together, and help them develop routines. For example, set up a study area where supplies are kept, and put books and materials away in a specific place so they are easy to find. We did a lot of our school work at the kitchen table, so we gave each student a crate for storing their books and supplies. Requiring them to be organized this way helped us avoid wasting excessive amounts of time trying to track down the needed resources.

Organization

Life is busy! Having your child make a weekly schedule is a very important organizational skill, and one that will serve them their whole life. When my children were younger, I managed the schedule completely. But starting in middle school, I began working with them on time management. First, we talked about what commitments they had or want to make time for, such as sports, activities, church, social, etc., and put them on the schedule. We then broke down their school work and determined a timeline for what needed to be done and when. By asking questions, I helped them think through how much time they needed for each subject. Do you need an hour a day for math? How much time will you need to read a book, write an outline and a rough draft? Next, I helped them to follow their schedule and tweak it as they better understood themselves and how much time activities really required. This process will help your child discover which subjects and activities take more time and which ones take less. They will also discover what are their more productive times during the day and what times are a wash.

A helpful practice is to front-load your week school-wise. That means overload the first couple days and then let the end of the week be lighter. This builds in a natural reward for working hard earlier and creates space for catching up if they don't get their work done. Try to have an activity day or schedule activities later in the afternoon so you can protect solid blocks for school-work. Otherwise your time will get away from you and it may become a battle to get things done. (This includes Mom's activities too. For example, most of my family lives out of town, so I talked on the phone often with my mom and sister. But I was careful to not call or receive calls until the afternoon. Simple adjustments like that made a world of difference in our schedule.) Make a schedule with them each week as long as they need you to help them. Time management is a difficult skill! Some children will learn this skill quickly, others may take a year or more. I have seen plenty of "smart" children fail due to being unorganized and many "average" students shine because of strong organization skills.

The skills of learning how to formulate, write and express ideas, break down tasks, pace work and organize a schedule are important abilities for which training begins in the middle school years. Your student will continue to develop these strengths throughout high school, and then they will serve them in whatever they do next.

Respect

Young adolescents have the ability to think and express complex thoughts, understand cause and effect and develop a stronger sense of right and wrong. When they were elementary age, they wanted you to tell them the answer (remember the queen of the castle?) Well, they still love you but, in their mind, your reign is over. Now they are beginning to test authority and ideas in general. They no longer just want to be told what to think. They want to "talk about issues and are eager to understand and make connections."[15] It is an important parenting and teaching skill to learn to listen and encourage your children to think through the "whys" of various issues. This is why reading good literature where characters make hard choices and face both good and bad consequences is important. Young teens have little life experience, but through the study of history and reading literature they can learn without having to pay the consequence themselves. Honestly, it is an exciting time to engage in conversation with your children. Ask lots of good questions so they can begin to refine their reasoning. You want them to develop the ability to think through issues and make good choices because their borders are expanding and you won't always be there to make the "right" decision for them.

This new independence and mental processing can also easily cross the line to disrespect, so it is a bit of a balancing act at times. Like any new skill, you need to train it. We have always encouraged our children to express their ideas and opinions but required they do so respectfully. That meant they had to have an appropriate tone and choose their words carefully. We did not allow them to speak disrespectfully about or towards their siblings, their friends or us. You have been teaching respect from the time they were toddlers, but as children get older their confidence and need to test truths becomes stronger and stronger. If you don't allow them the opportunity to talk through and wrestle the issues, but instead just tell them what to think, you may assume they agree with you but you will be shocked later when you find out they do not. By talking through their ideas, the conclusions they draw will be their own and will stick with them much more powerfully. The goal of open dialogue is to refine the thinking and reasoning required to arrive at well-founded conclusions. So this is a time for delving deeper into moral issues and for considering their desire for expanding freedoms and responsibilities.

Now, just to be clear, there are times to listen and process, and there are times that conclusions are not up for negotiation. You are still the parent and authority, which necessitates respect and obedience. There is a difference between processing their ideas and drawing conclusions that are disrespectful to God, family or others. While we are encouraging their thinking process at this stage, they need to know and honor limits and boundaries. We have sought to teach our children to obey first, and then ask questions. (As I said, finding this balance is not easy. I have not always done this well.)

Win Their Heart

You'll remember that we talked about nurturing the soul during the preschool and elementary years. In the middle school years, your goal is to win their hearts. Though your children are still dependent on you for the majority of their needs, they are growing in independence and beginning to develop their own identity. They still need parenting, but you'll want to lead without exasperating them. This is best accomplished by establishing clear, God-honoring boundaries that promote respect and trust, and by giving them a safe environment where they can learn to express themselves in a healthy manner. Usually, at this point in their development children still value their parent's approval, which can help motivate them to make good choices.

Parents of a Middle Schooler

As our children grow and change so do our lives as parents. A recent study by Suniya Luthar, Foundation Professor of Psychology at Arizona State University and Professor Emerita at Columbia University's Teachers College, found "that the years surrounding the onset of adolescence are among the most difficult times for mothers. During this period of transition, women can feel lonely, empty and dissatisfied with their mothering roles. The researchers also found that compared to mothers of infants, these women experience the lowest levels of maternal happiness and are even more stressed out than new parents."[16]

Personally, I did not feel lonely or empty at this stage. But that may have been due to my having other younger children, and the fact that our oldest was very loving toward me even as a middle schooler. But I add this because I agree that children grow and change, and many are not as responsive as they were when they were elementary aged. Their growing independence can be scary because, as a parent, you may feel like you have less control. There are a lot of issues to navigate, from the influence and managing of technology to the dynamics of relationships among friends and romantic interests. Adolescents can be moody and self focused and lash out their frustration on you, which is hurtful. But take heart, keep parenting. Middle schoolers need their parents as much as ever. They just may not be as good at showing it.

Conclusion

Homeschooling middle schoolers is more intensive academically than it was in elementary school, but you and your child are ready for it. You will continue to grow with them and build on what you have already accomplished. Young adolescents are dealing with lots of physical and emotional changes, as well as learning how to navigate friendship dynamics and a changing and often confusing culture.

I loved being there for my children during this time and felt homeschooling helped us to manage and simplify these many, necessary adjustments. Our relationships with each other were strong. As parents we remained the dominant voice in their lives, and home was a safe place. I am a firm believer that respecting their need to grow while continuing to parent during the middle school years has a great pay off in the high school years.

HIGH SCHOOL: 14-18 Years Old

Now we have reached my favorite season of homeschooling. By this time homeschooling is definitely a way of life. Students understand what is expected and the routines are pretty well established. (Although, that doesn't mean they will always follow them!) They are usually stronger at managing and completing their school work, emotions begin to even out, critical thinking is better developed and conversations are richer. Their unique interests and strengths become more evident, and it is fun to discover who they are as ones uniquely created by God. The freedom and flexibility of homeschooling at this level provides powerful opportunities to even further develop their emerging strengths.

Academics

You now have four years left. And, with your child's increasing knowledge, curiosity, and expanding social interests, it will be a jam-packed season that will go by quickly! So be especially mindful of your goals at this point, because there is a lot going on and it's easy to get caught in the business of it all. Your umbrella school will now be concerned about having the required number of credits in specific areas of study for graduation, and for going on to further education if desired. Requirements are outlined by your country or state regarding how many credits in English, history, math, science, etc. and electives are needed for graduation. You will make a transcript, or if you are under an umbrella school most of them will track your credits and manage your student's transcript. (It is not difficult to manage these requirements when the time comes, but the details are beyond the scope of this book.)

Use the first two years (freshman/sophomore) to hone skills and load academically. Remember the "front-load your week's work" principle, you will want to front-load your freshman and sophomore years with required subjects completing seven to eight credits. Then, during your junior and senior year, you can select subjects and opportunities more specific to your student's interests. This is helpful, given that by junior year students are often driving, working a part-time jobs and thinking about their post high school plans.

If your student is college bound, begin looking at colleges they may be interested in attending between their sophomore and junior year. Find out what those colleges are looking for in incoming freshman and adjust your high school program accordingly. Include internships, work studies and personalizing your student's experiences and opportunities. We did this with all our children and it was an incredible advantage. It is truly one of the major benefits of homeschooling.

Not All Academics

As you hopefully know by now, in my opinion American culture over emphasizes academics. Extensive focus during the teenage years is placed upon grades, standardized tests and what college to attend. Though working and making a living obviously matters, we've seen how limiting our focus to college entry during the high school years is a mistake. So is over committing our schedules to meaningless activities. Our children are most likely going to be spouses and parents, and are therefore going to need to be equipped to successfully manage their health, finances and families. So being strategic in using these years to develop the whole person is critical.

What are your child's unique interests and strengths? Seek ways to help develop them outside the traditional classroom through means such as travel, mission trips and volunteer work; look for internships and mentors. We took classes on topics like personal boundaries, finances and leadership. I know a family whose son was interested in mechanics. He spent a large portion of his junior year of high school building a motor from scratch. Our daughter took numerous mission trips to Honduras, with the opportunity for one of those trips arising in the middle of our

typical school schedule. The experience gained through inter-
acting with other cultures is invaluable, so we paused our routine
in order for her to go. Another opportunity came up for her to
travel to Italy during her senior year, a life long dream. She had
been saving for years in hopes of taking such a trip. It was a joy to
see her goal come to fruition as she reaped the benefit of her long-
term planning and diligent saving.

As mentioned earlier, our middle son Brooks loved music and
videography. So during his sophomore year we adjusted our
normal schedule to write, record and produce a full-production
music video parody called, "Monday". (*Google: Rebecca black -
Friday / Music Video Parody "Monday" by Brooks Barry.*) And
Pierz was interested in being a pastry chef, so we adjusted his
schedule to enable him to work four mornings a week for a sand-
wich shop for several months baking bread to see if it was really
something he wanted to pursue. We did numerous projects like
these throughout high school, tailoring the curriculum to our children's areas of special interest. Though not academic in the traditional sense, these experiences contributed greatly to our
children's application of knowledge in real-life settings. These are
fun years, and the opportunities are limitless!

Manage Freedom—You Are Still the Parent

Be aware that as your teenagers get older they become more and
more independent. You will see the addition of boyfriend and
girlfriend interest, part-time jobs and driver's licenses to name a
few. All are wonderful additions, and each new change has pros
and cons as you break new ground together! Your student
becomes more confident in their understanding and their views
on life. All this is good. But you are still the authority they need,
so don't stop parenting. Your teenagers may think they know best,
and that sometimes they know even more than you and therefore

do not need your guidance; but that, of course, is not true. In some ways they need you more than ever at this stage.

The expected responsibilities of adulthood are scary; the emotions of relationships in both friendships and dating, as well as figuring out how to make sense of a changing world, are immense. We homeschooled, were present and invested at all times, and it was still a challenge to navigate this stage and be on top of everything. To be really clear about this, we weren't always on top of everything, but we were present and engaged. So when issues came to light, having built a solid foundation throughout the earlier years really paid off. Our children trusted us, and we walked through some rough times together. Honestly, our children are going to make mistakes (so are their parents). So, during some of our challenges, after I got over the shock of what they had done, I was grateful they were still under our roof because we could walk through the repentance and learning process together.

They continued to mature and we definitely listened and considered their opinions and requests. However, just as in their junior high years, they were ultimately still under our authority and therefore needed to respect and honor it. I loved how Brett always told our children, "When you grow up and live on your own, you will have the freedom to make your own decisions. But, for now, you are under our roof and our rules, just as we are under God's."

Often parents of older teens seem to give up parenting. I don't know if they feel they can't require respect from their teens, or if they are just tired! I know some moms, particularly of teenage boys, stop parenting because it can be intimidating when you are 5'3 and your son is 6'4! (I love how one of my friends made her boys sit down in a chair when she corrected them in order to compensate for their height differences!) I too could sense the growing dynamic of our boys becoming young men, yet it was still my responsibility to hold them accountable. I want to take a minute and tell you a story about an incident that occurred with Brooks and how we handled it.

We were going through a transition time as a family. My husband is a worship pastor and had just accepted a new position at a different church in the area, and our family would now be attending the new church. We had been at the previous church for four years, so our children had a lot of friends. Brooks was almost 16 years old and it was the first Sunday in the new church. He was mad! Mad about leaving his friends and a thriving youth group. Mad because our new church had very few youth. Mad because he couldn't understand why we chose to leave. During worship, he was extremely agitated. With his frustration reaching a peak, he turned to me and said, "I can't be here." and then walked out.

Meanwhile, Brett was on stage leading worship! I couldn't very well interrupt him for backup, and I wasn't really sure what to do; but I had to deal with it.

I was sweating and praying as I followed Brooks out to the parking lot. He was angry! He vented his frustration and confusion, and I listened for a bit. Then I firmly and calmly told him I understood and that we could talk more about it later. But, for now, I needed him to come back into the sanctuary and participate by being present. I stated that we go to church as a family, it's only a few hours of his weekend and that we needed to support his dad. I really wasn't sure what he would do, or what I would do if he didn't come back in! But I knew I had to stay engaged and not just give in. It was tense!

Fortunately, Brooks gathered up his strength and self-control and came back in. He remained upset, but we got through that service.

Our teenage children grow in independence, but we must not stop parenting. And parenting works best when there is a solid foundation of respect and obedience that you continue to encourage and enforce. I admire Brooks for honoring me in that moment that day. He could have left, and some teenagers might have done just that. If he had, we would have had to still hold up the standard and implement consequences, and then work through that challenge together. My point is, at times you may feel like you're in way over your head in this parenting role. I sure have, and I definitely did that morning. But keep parenting! As hard as it is, your children need it. They want it. And the results are worth it.

Don't Stop Teaching

Similarly, don't stop teaching your student! You can hire tutors or use online classes and so on. But don't assume that your teenagers will become independent learners. Though students grow to become more and more capable and are able to personally manage more of their work load, their character isn't fully mature yet. They may not need you to directly teach in the same way you did when they were young, but they need you more than ever to process ideas with and to hold them accountable to complete assignments. I directed and monitored our children's school work consistently. (Maybe other people's children are more mature than mine. But if I hadn't remained engaged, they would still be working on Algebra 1!)

Conclusion

Homeschooling through high school allows a student the freedom to explore a vast array of opportunities because of the flexible schedule and yet still complete the academic requirements for graduation. As a parent, your role as leader, mentor and teacher continues to be of great importance, though it will be less hands on than it was when your children were younger. It is a privilege to homeschool your child through high school and to witness their growth and maturity while walking through the overall process together.

Long-Term Vision Benefits

Many of you reading this book may still have children who are barely school age, so it's hard to imagine them being able to dress themselves and get in the car independently, let alone think of them being teenagers and needing to manage their high school credits and emotions. But I wanted to give you a snapshot view of what each level can look like, and hopefully increase your vision of the long-term benefits of homeschooling.

Section 4

REFLECTIONS AT THE END OF THE JOURNEY

"Most People overestimate what they can do in one year and underestimate what they can do in ten years."

Bill Gates

I FEEL CALLED TO HOMESCHOOL

 "I feel called to homeschool...I hope it works."

Erin Barry

I was speaking to a group of parents of young children at a homeschool event. As I was sharing my heart, explaining why I believed in home education and why I knew they could be successful, I said "I feel called to homeschool... I hope it works!" I said it in the spirit of honesty and faith, much like I imagine the father pleading for Jesus to heal his son in Mark 9:24 might have felt: "...Lord, I believe; help my unbelief" (NKJV)! During the process of most things in life, we walk by faith; and homeschooling is no different. We fight our fears, the unexpected and the pressures to achieve the end goal. We hope and trust, but it is a risk! There are disappointments, successes, setbacks and surprises along the way. In this section, having successfully graduated all three of our children, I want to share some final reflections as a parent now sitting on the other side of homeschooling.

Suffering Produces Character

> Not only so, but we also glory in our sufferings, because we know that suffering produces perseverance; perseverance, character; and character, hope. And hope does not put us to shame, because God's love has been poured out into our hearts through the Holy Spirit, who has been given to us. Romans 5:3-5 (NIV)

I mentioned earlier that between Brett and I, I am the permissive parent. He was stricter and I was more lenient. We were careful to not let the children play us against each other, so we always remained a unified force. But there were times when I was at home alone with the children that I did not allow them to face the full consequence of their actions.

For example, if they didn't get their school work done because they were slacking off, I would give them more chances or cover for their shortcomings. Maybe I would help them meet a deadline on a subject or allow them another day to take a test when I should have let them fail. The poor grade or embarrassment of an incomplete assignment would not have had a long term effect on their schooling, but the failure would have had a huge effect on their character growth.

My lenience wasn't just regarding schoolwork either. Sometimes, I would not even punish them for disobedience. I gave them grace, at times, to a fault. Part of the problem was their pain was hard on me emotionally. In fact, it was often harder on me than on them.

For example, when leaving your children at Sunday school or some other childcare situation for the first time, have you ever had them scream and cry and grab at you for dear life? And, then after much agony, you finally leave traumatized and the whole time you're apart you feel awful? I have. And then, have you worried about them and emotionally beat yourself up for abandoning your sweet little ones, only to find that when you picked them up, though you're half expecting them to be in a devastated heap in the corner, to your surprise you learned that five minutes after you left they calmed down and ended up having a great time? And now they don't want to leave? Hard as it was, I learned that through these types of experiences they gain confidence, and once I recovered from shock, I was proud of them.

Obviously, there are exceptions, where a child doesn't cry or stop crying. But in most instances, children are resilient and have a great ability to adjust. The principle remains as they grow older. When our children are faced with pain we can carry it to an unhealthy degree, personally hurting much longer than they actually do. Or we can project emotions on them and add to the difficulty of the situation. I personally had to learn to separate myself emotionally and trust that even if they struggled at times it was okay, they were capable of adapting. Once I learned to assure them rather than overprotect them we both did better.

At other times, I'd let discipline slide because their consequence felt like punishment for me as well. It could mean losing out on something we were planning to do, or maybe I thought I'd look bad because of their weakness. I had to learn to find consequences where the children bore the weight of their disobedience, not me. And I had to be honest and acknowledge that they had sinful natures that we had to train. There is no shame in that!

Pain and consequences are excellent teachers. As I grew as a person and parent, I realized that by not letting my children face the consequences of their actions I was actually hurting them and denying them growth. If we coddle when we should confront, we produce immature, unprepared, young adults who don't learn responsibility and end up repeating their mistakes. But by experiencing the effect of their choices, a child gains the motivation to change. It is by working through our struggles that character is built.

The Bible talks about how suffering produces perseverance and perseverance, character, and character, hope. The funny part was that this letting them suffer not only grew their character, it grew mine. It reminded me I wasn't in control and that I had to trust God working in my children's lives to shape them too. One strategy that helped me was to prepare myself emotionally for their frustration when they were about to face the weight of the consequence of their actions. Preparing also helped me not step in and relieve them, but, rather, walk beside them as they learned.

Interestingly, when I let my children experience disappointment I discovered they became more responsible, capable and humble. At first, they reacted with anything from a sigh, to a huff, roll of the eyes, or pouting. Other times they expressed anger, blamed others, or cried. But as I calmly stood my ground and followed through, they eventually came to understand their weakness, and even apologized. They grew deeper in understanding of themselves, and the humility it produced was very powerful.

There are a lot of other by-products of stepping back and separating ourselves, but I want to briefly address three: autonomy, executive function, and healthy self-esteem.

The goal of parenting is to lead our children to autonomy by providing the nurturing and foundation for them to build healthy, independent lives. From childhood we are slowly training them through small tasks by letting them practice the skills they will need to be self-reliant. Honestly, the more times they fail at home, the better because we are there to mentor them through those situations. There will come a time when parenting stops. And we want our children to be confident and competent when that time comes.

Executive function is a term that former Dean of Freshmen at Stanford, Julie Lythcott-Haims, uses in her book, *"How to Raise an Adult: Break Free of the Overparenting Trap and Prepare Your Kid for Success."* It is the ability to problem solve, make decisions, face adversity and self-assert in order "to determine which goal-directed actions to carry out and when."[1] Lythcott-Haims states it is "developed through a mastery of basic problem-solving skills. Skills that are found in the everyday tasks of life: keeping your room clean, making yourself breakfast, remembering your own deadlines, and learning to self-advocate when things go wrong."[2] As a professor at Stanford, she goes on to state how, though each freshman class was more and more accomplished in academic skills, they lacked executive function and therefore couldn't make it on their own, ultimately relying on their parents to fix their problems. And these were college students!

Another side effect of lacking executive function was that "college students were more depressed, anxious and hopeless than ever before."[3] Handling problems and pushing through difficulties builds confidence and coping skills, which leads to healthy self-esteem.

Stephen R. Covey, in his book *The 7 Habits of Highly Effective People*, demonstrates how he and his wife learned the value of developing a healthy self-esteem while parenting their youngest son. He shares how they were too caught up in their son's performance and, though they were constantly verbally encouraging him and his competency, their actions were communicating the opposite, which exasperated his insecurity and awkwardness. Covey shares they had to learn "to stand apart – to separate us from him – and to [allow him to] sense his identity, individuality, separateness and worth."[4] Once they did that their son blossomed at his own speed and pace.

Your children are going to sin, lack wisdom, and mess up. As a parent, in order to help nurture their growth, you have to work at allowing them to face age appropriate consequences that may cause them to suffer. I finally realized my weakness and began working harder at letting them feel the pain of their bad choices and failures. As a result, I have grown in humility and dependence on the Lord, and I have seen my children's self-esteem, executive function and ultimately their independence grow.

I want to end with a quote that reminds us of the power of learning together in a family. "The Harvard Grant study (one of the longest studies of humans ever conducted) also found that happiness in life equals LOVE. Not passion, LOVE. Love of people and love of human experience. If there's anything that we can do for our kids, it's to teach them compassion, work ethic, and the love that can be found at home."[5]

The Value of Mentoring

Homeschooling encourages mentoring and offers smaller group settings, which are extremely beneficial. When I was a mother of young children, the majority of our church congregation (including the pastor) were about our age; between thirty and forty years old. Most of us had children who were about the same age, and much of our life experience was similar, too. During those years in Nashville, we made some incredible friends who are still dear to us today. Then, Brett accepted a worship director position at a church in Maryland that had a considerably broader demographic in their membership. I cannot tell you how much I benefited from the greater diversity of age and life experience, especially as a mother. I remember one friend who had three children that were spaced in age the same as mine, but five years older. Being able to see where we were headed parenting wise, and being able to glean from her insights as she reflected back to our stages, gave me not only helpful wisdom but great peace. Her mentoring, even though it was informal, influenced not only my parenting but my personal growth as well.

Homeschooling naturally incorporates mentoring by parent, other adults, and students. Since you learn as a family, you tend to connect with other families where your children are consistently among people of all ages. Throughout our lifetime, only in traditional school settings are we divided into classrooms where we interact solely with others our own age. One challenge with this, is that within any group, a leader usually emerges; and in a homogenous group, like a classroom, that leader is often the loudest or most aggressive, though not necessarily the wisest or most mature. But when there is age diversity, it is more likely that the emergent leader will be the more experienced and mature student of the group. Given the variety of settings a homeschool student may experience, the child can be a trainer in one instance and a trainee in another, depending on the situations they encounter. This is just one of the tremendous values in the cross-age exposure and relationships homeschooling offers.

Once again, I have talked with numerous parents over the years who are concerned that their children are missing out relationally by not being in the larger classroom settings that public school offers. I want to reiterate that being among more people, especially those of the same age, doesn't always mean you will develop better relationships. To the contrary, excessive peer-to-peer influence that is culturally driven can negatively affect the child's identity, whereas, the smaller groups, less peer time and intentional age and environment-diverse mentoring of home-schooling contributes significantly to their sense of well being.

As mentioned, in the typical school system students are with their peers for the majority of the day, making them the strongest influence in their lives. Homeschooling, while still availing plenty of time with peers, provides opportunity for deeper and more purposeful parent-student relationships, enabling the wisdom of adults to become the predominant voice in their lives. Even now, though our children are of college age, whether wrestling philosophies or making choices they still seek our input and guidance rather than only the opinion of their peers. To our delight, they also continue to seek the ongoing mentoring of other mature leaders.

Marriage and Homeschooling

If you are a married, homeschooling parent, it's important to keep in mind how impacting the marriage relationship is upon the healthy development of children. The natural tendency is to put our children first. You'll note that many if not most parents do this. However, while it makes sense, because we are responsible for their well being, our spouse needs to be and remain our first priority. My husband and I have a passion for helping strengthen marriages and families (see inseparablelives.com), so I want to share some thoughts regarding helping you keep your marriage strong.

A dear veteran homeschooling friend pulled me aside one day, and, with tears in her eyes confided the stress and strain she and her husband were wrestling within their relationship. They had been homeschooling for 16 years, having graduated two of their four children. The third was a senior and the youngest a sophomore. The children were thriving, but to her their marriage was dying. She confessed that she and her husband had little in common when the children weren't in the picture. She felt alienated and alone, and was devastated and scared. Sadly, they had nurtured their children but not their marriage. I wish her story was unique, but it's not. It is an easy place to gradually drift to. In our worthy pursuit of homeschooling we need to guard against focusing on our children at the cost of our marriage.

Balancing Children and Spouse

As homeschooling parents it is natural to spend time focusing on our children. After all, we have taken on the daunting task of being their prime educator. It is an enormous, time-consuming and vitally important job, but it means we have to intentionally and consistently work at setting and balancing our priorities. Otherwise, without even realizing it our children can take first place in our home. But that is not what God intended. Prioritizing our children is not healthy for them or our marriage. Actually, our children are best served when we put our marriage relationship first.

I remember being a young mother and first learning this truth. Our daughter Laurén was about 18 months old. She was adorable, but willful. Might I add, extremely willful. It was nap time, and Brett and I were excited to use the time to enjoy a quiet lunch date at home. Laurén did not like the idea and let us know through excessively high-decibel protests. She used grammar-stage tools to get her message across: duration, repetition, and intensity! I was torn. My heart ached to release her from her pain as she vocalized (screamed) from the other room. I remember Brett gently saying, "Erin, she is dry, she is fed, she is safe. Let her be. She needs to learn that we and our marriage are first. It was established before she came, and we will continue after she is grown and gone. She will be okay." I knew he was right, but my mother's heart yearned to satisfy my daughter. The first part of our lunch was not as quiet as we had anticipated, but she eventually gave in and went to sleep - and Brett and I had some much needed time together.

I realized that day how easy it was for me to put Laurén before our marriage. It would be something I would have to be deliberate about for years to come. But that day, I caught a glimpse of the truth of what Brett had said. Our marriage was established before she came and we would be the ones tending it after she had grown and gone. If I were to live 80 years, I could be married for 60 of those years but only have children in the home for 20-25 of them. This means our marriage could possibly encompass 35 years without children present. I began to see parenting and marriage in a whole new light. Honestly, I loved being a young mom. I loved how it fed me emotionally. But I knew I needed to be careful to establish proper priorities for meeting my emotional needs by putting God first, Brett second, and my children third.

Biblical Pattern of Acting Lovingly

The very nature of the parent-child relationship makes it easier to love our children than our spouse. Part of the reason is that we choose our spouse, but we receive our children. We choose our spouse for who they are, but also with an eye towards how they will improve our lives. We have certain expectations and our self-protecting nature tends to reward or love our spouse based on those expectations being filled. Timothy Keller in his book, *The Meaning of Marriage*, calls this a consumer relationship. This is because how we feel impacts how lovingly we act or don't act towards our spouse. Yet, we willingly accept our children and, regardless of what they do, we tend to act lovingly. Following is a summary outlining the process of how this happens.

Children are born extremely needy. They require attention around the clock. As parents we make tremendous sacrifices for them, with little reciprocation. As they grow they give more, but never to the degree that we as parents give to them. Then when they are teens, they may withdraw, rebel, or make mistakes that require enormous amounts of our time, resources, and investment, yet still give very little in return. "After eighteen years of this, even if your child is an unattractive person to everyone else, you can't help but love them dearly. Why? Because you've been forced to operate on the Biblical pattern. You have had to do the actions of love regardless of your feelings and therefore now have deep feelings of love for your child, however lovable he/she is or is not."[6]

Isn't that true? No matter the situation, we reap a deeply loving relationship when we operate by the Biblical instruction of choosing to act lovingly regardless of how we feel or are treated. Now consider the loving acts required of a homeschooling mother! They are multiplied by the extra time and focus home-schooling demands. As I said, I loved being a mother and home-schooling parent, and I delighted in acting lovingly towards my children. Of course, there is nothing wrong with that. But, recognizing these principles of relationship, I knew that in order for my marriage to remain strong and continue growing, I had to also ensure that I loved Brett through the Biblical pattern. That way our years as parents would not rob the intimacy of our relationship.

Putting It into Practice

Wherever you are today in your marriage, parenting and or homeschooling journey, I pray that you will consider these two perspectives: putting your marriage first and living the Biblical pattern of acting lovingly not only towards your children but also towards your spouse - regardless of how they act towards you. This will benefit your family both now and later. It is such a strange thing to consider that one day it will be back to just the two of you!

The Lord in His wisdom has made it so that, when our marriages are healthy, our children tend to be more content and well adjusted too. Isn't that our homeschooling goal? We want our children to have a great education but, more than that, we want them to be whole people who live out the full measure of God's intent for their lives. What a gift that is; when our priorities are balanced so are our families. Beautifully, God's alignment within the home benefits everyone.

Realignment

Fortunately, my veteran homeschooling friend and her husband, despite the emptiness and distance they felt, repented and began working towards rebuilding their marriage. They both began acting lovingly towards each other. They gave their marriage priority over their children. It took a few years but today, as their fourth child enters her senior year, they are growing stronger and closer as a couple. I am excited for them! Not only have they successfully launched their children, but as a couple they have demonstrated the power of true love and are now positioned to reap its benefits: a future together that will be rewarding and fulfilling.

My Kids

Surveying my 20 plus years of hindsight, do I still believe that homeschooling was the best choice for our children? My answer is a resounding, "Yes!"

I am so thankful we homeschooled. Each of our children have different strengths and weaknesses, but I believe they were educated and nurtured to their best potential. They are each creative, independent thinkers who express themselves well. They are comfortable with who they are, and they are each working out their salvation in the Lord. Would they have retained those strengths in public school? I don't know. But I do know that homeschooling certainly created an environment that encouraged and trained those skills.

Public school, by nature, compares children to each other. Students are ranked and assessed, and their value is determined by how they compare to the state standard. Our children were not sheltered from their struggles, but their struggles didn't define them. Brooks, as I shared, was behind academically until his senior year of high school. He had to work hard to be proficient at school, but that wasn't his identity. Homeschooling provided a safe place for him to work on his weaknesses. It allowed his academics to only be one part of his world, and not the defining part.

Pierz, our youngest son, is sharp. He would have done well in public school academically, but he was small physically and easily misunderstood. Would he have been bullied? Most likely. He was bullied enough at the neighborhood playground. Homeschooling allowed him to fully pursue his unquenchable desire to learn while giving him space to catch up physically and socially.

Our daughter Laurén was curious, creative and independent. Would public school have crushed those traits in an effort to push conformity? As it is, she was able to pursue her love for travel, dance and art and not compromise on her studies.

Where would they be spiritually? What would be the basis of their worldview? What would our family be like? Would they trust us like they do? Would they have the same relationship as siblings that they do now? I don't know. But I do know that homeschooling certainly helped establish those qualities that we so highly value.

Did homeschool cost them opportunities? No. They had a full life of experiences that extended well beyond the walls of a typical school education. They were all able to go to college and, even Brooks, my slow learner, ended up getting into Honors College. He did not test into Honors like his siblings did, but during his freshman year his English 101 professor took notice of him and said he belonged in Honors. He then personally walked him over to the department. What's interesting is that it was his interpersonal skills that distinguished him in the class, not his academic achievement. This is an important truth to note: Who we are weighs heavily into our opportunities. Obviously, he had to have the skills to do the work, but the relationships he built helped him get breaks that he otherwise would not have gotten.

Also, the transition to college was fairly smooth for all three of our children. As homeschoolers they attended outside classes once a week which required them to build the necessary organizational tools to manage their own assignments and deadlines, much like a college class expects. These skills served them well when they were given syllabuses in college and had to meet deadlines for assignments, papers and tests.

My children are still in process, and life will test them like it does all of us. We pray they stay true to the Lord. We pray they build strong families and live lives of integrity. But my window of parenting is over for the most part, and now we are moving into a relationship where my greatest influence will be more through prayer and friendship.

Beyond My Family

Are our children "homeschool poster kids"? Sort of a strange question, I know. But when writing a book about homeschooling there is almost this pressure to prove its value through what our experience has produced. But, children are people, not products. They have a free will. Our job is to introduce them to God through personal example, train them up in righteousness, and then release and encourage them to know and trust Him themselves.

Though I believe our children, and our whole family for that matter, have benefited tremendously from homeschooling, my reasons for promoting homeschooling are not because of the results of our family. As parents it is our responsibility to raise our children to the best of our ability; what they do with the tools and foundation we provided is up to them.

I will stand before the Lord at the end of my days and God will judge me for my choices, my obedience and my actions. Just as my children can't claim a relationship with the Lord through me, neither can I claim glory (or shame) for my adult children's actions. That's too much pressure on both the parents and the kids!

We must understand this separation or we can wrongly put our identity in who our children become. They will grow-up and become independent, and that is the way it should be. Of course, we remain in relationship with them, but it can be a struggle to fully release them, especially since we have put so much energy into their growth. A parent can almost feel like they have a right to how their children use what was given, but we don't.

Moral Fabric

Though we initially homeschooled because we believed it would give our children the best spiritual, emotional and educational foundation, as I continued to grow and learn I began to see a much bigger picture. Observing the rapid decline in the moral fabric of our culture, I realized that, along with developing our family, homeschooling was one of the most direct avenues for impacting the culture. I understood that a generation taught outside the system could contribute significantly to helping rebuild what has been lost. As parents, we hope our children will be part of that process. But we also understand that they ultimately make their own choices regarding what to do with what they've been given.

Regardless of where they go from here, I believe in homeschooling now more than ever. Our children's choices will not validate or invalidate us or the homeschool movement. I came to understand the reality of this truth a couple years ago when Laurén informed us about some things she had been walking through of which we were unaware.

I was to speak at a homeschool conference on a Monday. The Saturday before, Laurén had just told Brett about her struggles with her faith, and choices she had been making throughout the process. We all make wrong choices, and though I was deeply grateful she would come and talk with us, I was devastated and felt disqualified to represent the value of homeschooling because of where she was in her faith and the direction she appeared to be heading. I felt responsible. I felt like I had failed. She was successful in university, in work and in many other areas. But, for me, her faith was the most important aspect of her life and a major reason for my homeschooling her. Where had I gone wrong?

Interestingly, God gave me a dream that Sunday night. In it He showed me the truth once again—that I am responsible for my actions, not hers. We had done our part, obeying Him by home-schooling our children the way He had instructed us and giving them the knowledge of Truth. We had to entrust her to Him, knowing she was still in process. She was now a young adult, and my responsibility was to pray and let her work out her relation-ship with the Lord. I could speak confidently about home-schooling and yet humbly share the truth of where we were at. She was not my badge of success; neither was she my mark of fail-ure. She was not the indicator of whether homeschooling was valuable or not. We could rest in the fact that she had a solid foundation of Biblical truth. We had to release her and pray and trust that she would choose to build on what we had imparted.

Today, I am grateful to God to be able to report that she worked through those challenges and is in a beautiful place in her walk with the Lord. I am extremely thankful. But she proved once again, as each of us likely have to our parents at one time or another, that the battle for the souls of our children is fierce! There are no guarantees. But, even so, we must do our best to raise a generation who can not only think and express themselves well, but who love God and desire to please Him. With our current pluralistic culture, a Biblical worldview is not going to be the foundation of a public school education or forum. Home-schooling is one way to ensure that our children are at least taught and mentored in Christ-centered values. I am confident that God is raising a generation firmly grounded in the truth of Scripture for such a time as this, and I am excited to be a part of encouraging and equipping parents in this journey.

None of My Fears Became Reality

I had so many fears when I started! Fears about my limitations, fears about specific subjects, fears about my children's weak-nesses, fears about their future and mine! Yet, not one of them came to pass. I definitely had limitations, but I grew during the process of teaching. My children had limitations, but we faced them as a family. We had financial and health and life problems along the way. There were years where money was very tight, which meant we had to be extremely creative with our books and supplies. One year I was diagnosed with Lyme disease and taught many days from bed. Another year, our son was diagnosed with Type I Diabetes, which was traumatic and life-changing. I could share story after story of how we faced and overcame difficulties, and struggles, and how God met us every step of the way. I praise God we didn't let our fear, or limitations, keep us from trying.

Final Thoughts

"The days are long but the years are short." I think that quote sums it up for me. I remember wondering as a young mother if I would ever get to sleep a whole night or go to the bathroom alone; and now, here I am at the end of my in-home, homeschooling journey. (I say it that way because I will continue working with other parents and the homeschool world.) Pierz graduated May 2016. For the last few years, obviously, I saw this day coming. Although it's strange, it still felt a bit shocking when I realized we were in our last year. It's so easy to get caught up in the fullness of life. You're moving along in the muchness of the every day; then, suddenly, you look up one day and you are standing with three grown children. Indeed, the days are long, but the years are short. I can't believe that season is finished. Where did the time go?

I've always wondered how I would feel when we finished. Would I feel relieved? Would I feel lost? Tired? Proud? But, surprisingly, my overwhelming emotion has been gratitude. I am so grateful to the Lord that He sustained us. That, in His faithfulness, He actually enabled us to complete the process.

Like anything, our homeschooling wasn't perfect. I look back and, with my experience now, there are things I think I would do differently because I have matured in both my teaching ability and as an adult. And yet, without our mistakes, we wouldn't have learned all we did. We wouldn't be where we are today. Somehow, God used it all and made something beautiful.

The other day, Pierz came home from his college calculus class. He said, "Mom, my professor is really hard to follow. We have a test coming up and I need to study. Can you spend an hour with me later today to make sure I am doing this right? Would 4:00 work?"

Inside, I laughed to myself with great delight. Wasn't this the child I had to constantly say, "Is your math done? Let me see your outline for your paper! It's due tomorrow and you have how much done!? And now only a few months later, he is so responsible and booking time with a tutor (me) because he has a test coming and wants to make sure he is prepared. I agree to the request. (Plus, I thought, "He has a job now, so he can afford my rates!")

It's now 4:00 PM, and we sit once more at the kitchen table. I look at him with his graphing calculator and college syllabus, and I have to fight back the tears. Not because I miss the days gone by, our homeschooling season is over and we lived it to the fullest of our ability. Rather, I am thankful he would ask me for help and that I get these few extra moments. I love sitting with him, and I treasure our time together. I remember all the lessons we shared at this table, from basic addition and letters and sounds to the intricacy of human cells and discussions of governments and wars. We have been study partners for a long time.

All in all, I can't help but marvel at who Pierz is becoming, and at God's goodness to our family. I have peace in my heart because, though our homeschooling days weren't perfect, we spent them together and we can now clearly see the value of having remained committed to the journey.

We work a few problems and I can see that he is lacking a little confidence. He quickly finds his stride. He doesn't need me in that capacity anymore, as the skills and foundation have been laid. He, like his sister and brother, is ready. Ready to test and refine all that has been sown.

As I leave the table, he lets me kiss him gently on the forehead.

He continues working.

My heart soars.

May God be glorified.

～

APPENDIX I — PLURALISM AND SOCIALIZATION

First, let me clarify, that I am addressing philosophy in education in this section, not people. I have taught in the public, private, and homeschool arena for over 30 years. I have been a preschool, elementary, Jr High, High School teacher, and an adjunct College Professor. The professionals I have had the privilege of working with in all these schools were devoted, highly-skilled individuals for whom I have the utmost respect and who constitute some of my dearest friends. So I, like you, value teachers and education.

My concern, however, is that our trust of teachers may lead to an equal trust of the system. Sometimes we don't realize that, along with academics, schools teach our children values and norms. At first glance, this might seem fine. But a deeper look should cause us pause—especially where the values and norms are in conflict with our own.

We live in a pluralistic culture, which is defined by Dictionary.com as "a conviction that various religious, ethnic, racial, and political groups should be allowed to thrive in a single society."[1]

Pluralism is a highly held value of the United States and one we work hard to maintain. But when it comes to education, the idea of pluralism breaks down. If public school is to serve everyone, then how is it possible to not offend some beliefs? Clearly, it is not possible, because many of the various religious, ethnic, racial, and political beliefs are contradictory. Theoretically, the way to manage a pluralistic environment is through neutrality. However, neutrality can never really be the result because, when you have opposing views, any concrete decision will offend one side other the other. For example, our schools are very secular. Students or teachers with opposing religious views are required to keep their opinions to themselves. For Christians, then, this is at the expense of their principles. Later, in Appendix III, I share some Supreme Court rulings that put limits on the absolutes that are allowed to be taught or discussed in the public school system.

So what do we do if the values and norms being taught in public school are in conflict with our own? As we discussed, wouldn't the one-sided approach lead to negative socialization, or worse, influence a secular mindset in our children? Do we have a recourse in the public system? If not, what are our options? These are some of the hard questions we have to ask ourselves when making educational decisions for our children.

Education Is Biased

Education is not neutral. Education by its very nature is biased. In discussions of education the case is often made to separate fact and opinion. There is a philosophy that children shouldn't be taught morals, but that they should be left to decide them for themselves. The argument goes something like this, "If we just deal with facts, then no morals will be attached." In this way, no one is imposing their ideas on others. But how far does that really get us? Let's consider Christopher Columbus. We can say that in

1492 he sailed the ocean blue. A small child may be satisfied with that fact. But an older school aged child's next question is going to be, why? That moves beyond just fact to interpretation. It includes assumptions and judgements regarding those assumptions, which has to include morals.

I know this firsthand because I took American History at university in Canada. When I moved to the States (after I married a great American man!), I got a teaching job, which included teaching American History. I must confess that the American History curriculum I was expected to teach from had a totally different take on a number of facts than what I had been taught in university. I was confused, so I did some research. I came to the conclusion that my professor's interpretation was the incorrect one (which shouldn't have been a surprise since he was an open Communist!). So, of course, his Marxist philosophy influenced his presentation of the United States. Sadly, having no other reference for the material he taught (I took American History in high school but it was general and limited), I took his word for it and didn't realize the bias until I began teaching it myself.

Why was I taking history from a Communist in the first place, you ask? Good question and it makes my point here complete. I went to university to become a teacher. Everyone who wanted to be a teacher went to university. That was the process. I got into my provincial university that had a respected, certified program. The school laid out the requirements for the degree. One of the first required classes was a history, so I chose the one from the course catalog that fit my schedule. I never questioned the professor, content or requirement. I assumed that the university was the expert and I could trust what they offered. The idea that an ideology along with the course material might be part of the teaching method never crossed my mind. I willing accepted the content, how it was presented, and, very importantly, how it was interpreted. After all, it was my first year, first semester, and my professor was the authority.

In university, the process for assessment was still to regurgitate what was being taught, instead of being encouraged to reason, process information, and then draw conclusions. In short, I was still being told what to think. And because of my lack of foundational information in American History (and the need for a grade), I didn't discern the bias. I had been educated in the system and was a good product of it. I did not ask questions. There wasn't time, nor was it encouraged.

The university determined the academics and the standards, which included the philosophies associated with the content. While this was not exclusive to history, the example from my history class illustrates the truth of the matter.

We are aware (usually) of the blatant discrepancies in philosophy, but what about the more subtle ones? I was 17 years old and better prepared to sift through the ideas, and yet I was affected unaware. What about young children? Douglas Wilson speaks to this point in his book, *Recovering The Lost Tools of Learning*. He shares how he, having been educated in the public schools, remembered obvious philosophies in high school where "he was conscious of the conflict between what he learned at home and what he learned at school." Wilson continues,

 "...as I have grown in my adult understanding of the Christian faith, I have become increasingly aware of conflicts I did not recognize as a child – conflicts at the level of presuppositions. I have had to unlearn many things."[2]

The good news is that the author recognized the conflict and realigned his thinking with Scripture. But is that a risk we want to take with our children? Our current public school graduates are

very secular. "Young people today are not only more religiously unaffiliated than their elders; they are also more religiously unaffiliated than previous generations of young people ever have been as far back as we can tell," [Pew Sr. Researcher] Greg Smith tells NPR Morning Edition co-host David Greene."[3]

As stated, our culture is pluralistic. The goals and philosophies supported by the school system directly affect what is taught, what is measured, and ultimately what is produced. To produce people that support the status quo involves a different education than one that produces people who think critically, challenge the status quo, and affect change. How did the millennial generation become so secular? Obviously, the education system alone cannot be blamed for that, but neither can its influence be excluded from the mix.

I didn't fully understand when I was in university that there could be an agenda in education that conflicted with my beliefs or that it might affect my presuppositions or how I might think. Like most people, I trusted the system unquestioningly. I was raised in it. It was familiar. It was the norm. But we need to ask the question, "How do I want my children to be socialized?" Is there an objective, absolute standard? And who decides what the standard or philosophy of their education should be? Between the parent and state, who knows my child best or really has their best interests in mind?

Once our children are in school we transfer a lot of our authority to the system, which directly affects what and how they think. So what I am trying to emphasize here is that, before we place our children in the public school system, we consider that the system determines the content and values taught and that those ideas are embedded in the curriculum, methods, attitudes, and environment with regards to its socializing agenda and pluralistic philosophy. And ultimately, to help us to recognize that, though the unknown aspects of homeschooling can make us nervous, the pluralistic aspects and effect of government education should cause us even greater concern.

Again, the direct and intentional mentoring of our children throughout their educational years is necessary to not only their health as individuals, but to the well being of society as a whole.

APPENDIX II — COMPULSORY PUBLIC EDUCATION

Why do we send our children to public school? For most of us this is what we were born into. Our parents went to school; we went to school, so we send our children to school. That is the way we've always done it. Or is it? Let's consider a very brief summary of some of our own nation's history of public education. American Public School is a newer concept, has had a number of purposes/agendas associated with it over the years and as we consider American public education's history it sheds some new light on the idea of socialization.

One of the earliest records of public education in the United States is in the mid-1600s from the New England Puritans. Their purpose in establishing public education was to promote the Bible. They had a law as early as 1647 that required a township with fifty householders or more to appoint a person to teach all the children literacy so they could read the Bible. The Bible was the number one selling book in the American colonies. The second was the New England Primer, which was their foundational school text. "It [the New England Primer] was a small book filled with alphabets, lessons, verses, prayers and the Westminster Catechism."[1]

So the curriculum they used to teach basic skills was heavily indoctrinated in Protestant principals for a reason. These early settlers had come to America to avoid religious persecution and they established their colonies on religious uniformity. They knew in order to ensure their beliefs and philosophies be established and continued they'd need to use the socializing power of education to pass on the norms and values they believed in. Thus their schools and curriculum were formed and crafted for that reason.

Many people played a role in the philosophy of education. One of the leading voices in the 1830's was Horace Mann. "He is often credited with leading the Common School Movement, which helped to lay the framework for a publicly funded education system."[2] Driven by his limited education opportunities as a child he tried to compensate through "the Common School Movement [by] pushing for a better developed, tax-funded secular public school system."[3] He began a bi-weekly publication to help reshape how public education was perceived, began training institutes for teachers "aimed at preparing teachers by establishing pedagogical norms and standards."[4] He established his teacher education through his Six Guiding Principles.

After the Civil War the country "was faced with the huge task of rebuilding itself"[5] and unifying the nation to counter the division the war caused. Education played an enormous role in establishing equality for the newly freed, uneducated slaves and trying to reinforce a peaceful norm.

 "The Freedmen's Bureau was a first step in the goal of equality. It was put together by the federal government to help freed slaved and refugees transition to freedom and the new society the South faced after the Civil War... Before the Civil War, no Southern state had an established system of public schools...by the end of 1865 (the first year the Bureau operated), there were more than 90,000 freed slaves enrolled in public school. The establishment of free schools for former slaves impacted education in many ways. One major way that it changed the landscape of education was by espousing [promoting] a belief in and commitment to the idea that everyone can and should be educated. As more and more people attended public schools, states began to take notice and establish free public schools for everyone, black and white."[6]

Sadly there were extremely turbulent years between the Civil War and the Civil Rights Movement with rulings that supported segregation. But ultimately, the commitment to the idea that everyone can and should be educated was established.

In 1870 the first federalized U.S. education board the NEA (National Education Administration) was formed. Among other reasons one driving purpose was to establish certain foundational beliefs. They quickly announced that countrywide school science courses must be restructured to teach "evolution" as fact, not theory. A new move toward secular thinking was deliberately promoted by the public schools.

John. D. Rockefeller, a member of NEA, having gained a fair amount of pull in the association, created the GEB (General Education Board) in 1903 with a similar agenda. Any doubt regarding the Rockefeller's intent in starting the GEB should be clarified in John D's own mission statement:

     "In our dreams, people yield themselves with

perfect docility to our molding hands. The present education conventions of intellectual and character education fade from their minds, and, unhampered by tradition, we work our own good will upon a grateful and responsive folk... The task is simple. We will organize children and teach them in a perfect way the things their fathers and mothers are doing in an imperfect way."[7]

This quote suggests that the purpose of public education at the turn of the century was a means to raise a working class to suit the growing needs of American Industry leaders.

In 1918, every state required students to complete elementary school.

Other quotes indicate that the purpose of some curriculum was to impart specific ideologies. "1968: Edith Roosevelt's Article, *The Foundation Machine* indicts Carnegie Funded Textbooks. Carnegie-funded "Programmed Textbooks" were distributed to "culturally deprived areas." Edith Roosevelt stated that

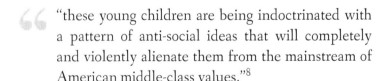

"these young children are being indoctrinated with a pattern of anti-social ideas that will completely and violently alienate them from the mainstream of American middle-class values."[8]

Ms. Roosevelt's article suggests once again, that American public education had a specific socializing intent teaching and much more than just the basic skills, reading and writing.

In the 1960's and 1970's the emphasis of "STEM" education was driven by the space race.

In 1979 the Department of U.S. Education was founded.

Next, President Reagan talked about bringing some previously held values back into school, such as prayer, which had been removed in 1962. George W. Bush signed the No Child Left Behind Act in 2002 in an effort to develop and assess national standards. And most recently, the Common Core Curriculum was developed with the rational

> "that America couldn't lead the world in innovation and remain being competitive if we didn't have an internationally competitive education system,...the entire purpose of the standards, ... was to determine what students need to know and demonstrate the ability to do in order to be prepared for an entry-level college course."[9]

Though the Common Core may have begun with the push for a competitive education system, the content of the Common Core was established after the initial rational and its philosophical and political bend cannot be denied. I would strongly advise you to read about its contents. In addition to the political aspect, there is sexual content and other ideologies you need to be aware of should you choose to use the public system.

When we look at compulsory education in the above brief mixture of facts, we realize two things: First, government controlled and authorized compulsory education is a relatively new idea. It has only been mandated in the United States for the last hundred years or so. That is not very long. And secondly, it indicates that along with the academic skills, education is a way to pass on values and beliefs, and man has known that and used it.

> "Up until the 1840's, the American school system was mainly private, decentralized, and

homeschooling was common. Americans were well educated and literacy rates were high."[10]

Considering just the facts we've presented here, the American Public School System has promoted religious values, national unity, racial rights, the development of a working class, secular beliefs, generational separation and political agendas. All under the guise of teaching the subjects of reading, writing and arithmetic!

America is not alone in understanding the power of propagating through education. Look at the following quotes from a number of international leaders, who have recognized the natural relationship and benefit of combining education and ideology.

Adolf Hitler said, "He alone, who owns the youth, gains the future."[11]

Abraham Lincoln said, "The philosophy of the school room in one generation will be the philosophy of government in the next."[12]

Joseph Stalin said, "Education is a weapon whose effect depends on who holds it in his hands and at whom it is aimed."[13]

The Lord God said, "Train up a child the way he should go and when he is old he will not depart from it" Prov 22:6 (NKJV).

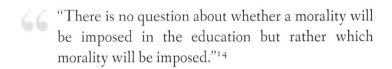

"There is no question about whether a morality will be imposed in the education but rather which morality will be imposed."[14]

So homeschooling is a trusted, long standing form of education and socialization, and attending a "school" is a relatively modern idea.

APPENDIX III — SUPREME COURT RULINGS

Since we are a pluralistic society, our public schools lean towards secular views over religious ones, and, in order to compensate for disparate ideas and ideals, have opted to ban most Judeo-Christian beliefs as unconstitutional. Consider some of the Supreme Court decisions, followed by their dates of enactment, regarding the legal restrictions that affect religion in public education.

McCollum v. Board of Education Dist. 71, 333 U.S. 203 (1948) — Court finds religious instruction in public schools a violation of the establishment clause and therefore unconstitutional.

Burstyn v. Wilson, 72 S. Ct. 777 (1952) — Government may not censor a motion picture because it is offensive to religious beliefs.

Engel v. Vitale, 82 S. Ct. 1261 (1962) — Any kind of prayer, composed by public school districts, even nondenominational prayer, is unconstitutional government sponsorship of religion.

Abington School District v. Schempp, 374 U.S. 203 (1963) — Court finds Bible reading over school intercom unconstitutional and Murray v. Curlett, 374 U.S. 203 (1963) - Court finds forcing a child to participate in Bible reading and prayer unconstitutional.

Epperson v. Arkansas, 89 S. Ct. 266 (1968) — State statue banning teaching of evolution is unconstitutional. A state cannot alter any element in a course of study in order to promote a religious point of view. A state's attempt to hide behind a nonreligious motivation will not be given credence unless that state can show a secular reason as the foundation for its actions.

Lemon v. Kurtzman, 91 S. Ct. 2105 (1971) — Established the three part test for determining if an action of government violates First Amendment's separation of church and state:

1) the government action must have a secular purpose;

2) its primary purpose must not be to inhibit or to advance religion;

3) there must be no excessive entanglement between government and religion.

Stone v. Graham, 449 U.S. 39 (1980) — Court finds posting of the Ten Commandments in schools unconstitutional.

Wallace v. Jaffree, 105 S. Ct. 2479 (1985) — State's moment of silence at public school statute is unconstitutional where legislative record reveals that motivation for statute was the encouragement of prayer. Court majority silent on whether "pure" moment of silence scheme, with no bias in favor of prayer or any other mental process, would be constitutional.

Edwards v. Aquillard, 107 S. Ct. 2573 (1987) — Unconstitutional for state to require teaching of "creation science" in all instances in which evolution is taught. Statute had a clear religious motivation.

Allegheny County v. ACLU, 492 U.S. 573 (1989) — Court finds that a nativity scene displayed inside a government building violates the Establishment Clause.

Note a school is a government building.

Lee v. Weisman, 112 S. Ct. 2649 (1992) — Unconstitutional

for a school district to provide any clergy to perform nondenominational prayer at elementary or secondary school graduation. It involves government sponsorship of worship. Court majority was particularly concerned about psychological coercion to which children, as opposed to adults, would be subjected, by having prayers that may violate their beliefs recited at their graduation ceremonies.

"US Supreme Court Decisions. "The Secular Web. Secular Coalition of America, 2016. Web. 8 July 2016."[1]

These are only a handful of rulings but it demonstrates the philosophical bend of public education, which excludes and views as a violation what I see as the necessary foundation of a good education.

APPENDIX IV — NEA RESOLUTIONS

These are a few resolutions from the 2015- 2016 resolutions of the NEA, The National Education Association. You will see the resolutions also support our nation's pluralistic views. The document is massive and there are a plethora of resolutions regarding numerous topic areas, all of which will impact the curriculum and emphasis. Many are good resolutions. I am pointing out some that I consider worth knowing when weighing the overall philosophies our children would be under if attending public government schools. I have shortened some of the resolutions and emphasized those I thought were worth noting. But you can read the entire pdf (2016 Resolutions Summary) at the following URL: ra.nea.org.

"A-34. Federally or State-Mandated Choice/Parental Option Plans The Association believes that federally or state-mandated parental option or choice plans compromise free, equitable, universal, and quality public education for every student. Therefore, the Association opposes such federally or state-mandated choice or parental option plans."

B-12. Diversity The National Education Association believes

that a diverse society enriches all individuals. Similarities and differences among race, ethnicity, color, national origin, language, geographic location, religion, gender, sexual orientation, gender identity, age, physical ability, size, occupation, and marital, parental, or economic status form the fabric of a society. Education should foster a vibrant, pluralistic society that authentically reflects diverse populations and cultural perspectives.

B-14. Racism, Sexism, Sexual Orientation, and Gender Identity Discrimination The National Education Association believes in the equality of all individuals. Discrimination and stereotyping based on such factors as race, gender, sexual orientation, gender identity, disability, ethnicity, immigration status, occupation, and religion must be eliminated. The Association also believes that plans, activities, and programs for education employees, students, parents/guardians, and the community should be developed to identify and eliminate discrimination and stereotyping in all educational settings. Such plans, activities, and programs must

a. Increase respect, understanding, acceptance, and sensitivity toward individuals and groups.

b. Eliminate discrimination and stereotyping in curricula, textbooks, resource and instructional materials, activities, etc.

c. Foster the dissemination and use of nondiscriminatory and non-stereotypical language, resources, practices, and activities

d. Eliminate institutional discrimination

e. Integrate an accurate portrayal of the roles and contributions of all groups throughout history across curricula, particularly groups that have been underrepresented historically

f. Identify how prejudice, stereotyping, and discrimination have limited the roles and contributions of individuals and groups, and how these limitations have challenged and continue to challenge our society.

g. Eliminate subtle practices that favor the education of one student over another on the basis of race, gender, sexual orientation, gender identity, disability, ethnicity, or religion

h. Encourage all members of the educational community to examine assumptions and prejudices, including, but not limited to, racism, sexism, and homophobia, that might limit the opportunities and growth of students and education employees

i. Offer positive and diverse role models in our society, including the recruitment, hiring, and promotion of diverse education employees in our public schools

j. Coordinate with organizations and concerned agencies that promote the contributions, heritage, culture, history, and special health and care needs of diverse population groups.

k. Promote a safe and inclusive environment for all. The Association encourages its affiliates to develop and implement training programs on these matters. (1996, 2015)

B-30. Educational Programs in Support of Lesbian, Gay, Bisexual, Transgender, and Questioning Students The National Education Association supports appropriate and inclusive educational programs that address the unique needs and concerns of lesbian, gay, bisexual, transgender, and questioning (LGBTQ) students. The Association also supports efforts and contributions by educators, parents/guardians, community leaders, organizations, and partners in the development of these programs. Specific programs should provide

a. Acknowledgement of the significant contributions of diverse LGBTQ persons in American history and culture

b. Involvement of educators knowledgeable in LGBTQ issues in the development of educational materials that integrate factual information about the history, social movements, and current events of LGBTQ people.

c. Developmentally appropriate local, state, and national resources. (2015)

B-53. Sex Education The National Education Association

believes that the developing child's sexuality is continually and inevitably influenced by daily contacts, including experiences in the school environment. The Association recognizes that sensitive sex education can be a positive force in promoting physical, mental, emotional, and social health and that the public school must assume an increasingly important role in providing the instruction. Teachers and health professionals must be qualified to teach in this area and must be legally protected from censorship and lawsuits. ...programs should include information on—

a. Sexual abstinence, birth control, family planning, prenatal care, parenting skills, the effects of substance abuse during pregnancy, and the issues associated with pre-teen and teenage pregnancy

b. Diversity of culture and diversity of sexual orientation and gender identity

c. Sexually transmitted diseases, incest, sexual abuse

B-82. Homeschooling The National Education Association believes that homeschooling programs based on parental choice cannot provide the student with a comprehensive education experience. When homeschooling occurs, students enrolled must meet all state curricular requirements, including the taking and passing of assessments to ensure adequate academic progress. homeschooling should be limited to the children of the immediate family, with all expenses being borne by the parents/guardians. Instruction should be by persons who are licensed by the appropriate state education licensure agency, and a curriculum approved by the state department of education should be used. The Association also believes that home-schooled students should not participate in any extracurricular activities in the public schools. The Association further believes that local public school systems should have the authority to determine grade placement and/or credits earned toward graduation for students entering or re-entering the public school setting from a homeschool setting. (1988, 2006)

I-17. Family Planning The National Education Association believes in family planning, including the right to reproductive freedom. The Association also believes the government should give high priority to making available all methods of family planning to women and men unable to take advantage of private facilities. The Association further believes in the implementation of community-operated, school-based family planning clinics that will provide intensive counseling by trained personnel. (1985, 2015)

I-25. Freedom of Religion The National Education Association believes that freedom of religion is a fundamental human right. The Association also believes that choice of religion is an intensely personal decision. Instruction in religious doctrines and practices is best provided within a family setting and/or by religious institutions. The Association further believes that schools should teach the rights and responsibilities associated with the freedom of religion, the religious heritage and diversity of the United States, respect for the beliefs of others, and the historical and cultural influences of various world religions. The Association believes that local school boards should adopt policies that govern religious activities on school property. Such policies must respect the separation of church and state; govern voluntary, student-led meetings with adult supervision before or after normal school hours; treat all religions on an equal basis; and protect the rights of students and education employees. The Association also believes that the constitutional provisions on the establishment of and the free exercise of religion in the First Amendment require that there be no sectarian practices in the public school program. The Association opposes the imposition of sectarian practices in the public school program and urges its affiliates to do the same. The Association also opposes any federal legislation or mandate that would require school districts to schedule a moment of silence. The Association particularly opposes a moment of silence as a condition for receiving federal funds. (1995, 2008)

I-51. Hate-Motivated Violence The National Education Association believes that acts or threats of hate-motivated violence, including, but not limited to, physical and verbal violence against individuals or groups because of their race, color, national origin, religion, gender, sexual orientation, gender identity, age, disability, size, marital status, or economic condition are deplorable. The Association also believes that federal, state, and local governments and community groups must oppose and eliminate hate-motivated violence and that current events and/or economic conditions should not diminish such opposition. (1991, 2015)

I-22 Marriage Equality. "The National Education Association believes in marriage equality for all individuals. Discrimination and stereotyping based on such factors as race, gender, sexual orientation, gender identity, disability, ethnicity, immigration status, occupation, and religion must be eliminated."[1] NEA Handbook / NEA 2015 Convention Resolutions

If you read all the resolutions of the NEA, honestly, it is overwhelming to consider the number of issues included as part of their mandate. It is jam packed with social issues.

One final quote in this section, noting the social and political focus of government education, is taken from an article from HSLDA (homeschool Legal Defense Association) called, Common Core Math Strives Toward Goal of "Social Justice." The article discusses the addition of social justice to the teaching of math by the National Council for Teachers of Mathematics (NCTM).

 "NCTM is able to incorporate politically charged

lessons into Common Core math curriculum on its open-source curriculum platform, Illuminations. In a lesson about election results titled, *How Could That Happen*, students in fourth grade are asked whether or not the 2000 election was fair. Students are given the opportunity to explore the mathematical questions in a politically challenging context. The answer key instructs teachers, 'The written answer should extend beyond the given math problem and use the math to reflect on context.'"[2]

The purpose of current government education is religiously restricted by the laws of the land, influenced by the resolutions of the NEA and combines political propaganda under the influence of the NCTM and Common Core, which adds focuses to the curriculum that we didn't want to be a part of our children's education. Not only do the many social issues distract from learning, the absence of Biblical absolutes is counter intuitive to character development.

Ultimately, these restrictions limit the ideas students are exposed to and denies them the critical dialogue necessary for the development of higher level thinking and personal growth.

Education Influences Social Identity

In social identification, "we adopt the identity of the group we have categorized ourselves as belonging to."[3] If we are passing on "the soul of a society,"[4] then the student's identity (who they are based on who or what they identify with) is going to be part of the outcome of their education. In any education there will be social qualities that are valued. Those values will be communicated and praised, and the opposite, conflicting qualities will be discouraged and vilified. Notice that tolerance is a value communicated and praised by the NEA. In the government school system, students will therefore be taught tolerance (according to the government's definition); they will be rewarded for being tolerant and punished for being intolerant. For example, a current value being asserted under tolerance is gender neutrality. Since the governments wants our population to assimilate this value, the schools are implementing programs, curriculum and regulations in support of it. By affiliation with these values, gender neutrality will become common place. It is what they will be taught, what they will practice and what will be praised. It will become the norm and form part of their social and group identity.

The latest Pew Research notes that 25% of the population now identifies as religiously unaffiliated. One half of the religious "nones," people who don't affiliate with any religion, were raised in religion. Two of their main reasons for leaving religion are their lack of belief and science. Considering the emphasis on science and the removal of all religious answers, are these results surprising?

The current generation of students has the most secular mindset we have ever seen in the history of America, and the education they have received has heavily influenced them. The school system defined anything to do with the Bible or Christianity, such as the 10 Commandments and praying and/or teaching creation, as unconstitutional, and the result is a generation without a belief in God. As one Millennial in the pew research said, "I'm a scientist now."[5]

Children attend school for seven hours a day, 180 days a year for thirteen years, not including college. That is a lot of time under a philosophy that may be at best different from yours and, at worst, virtually opposite. Government schools are a great success, as the majority of students who graduate from them believe and value what they have been taught. As a result many are walking away from their faith.

For example, "using a sample size of 9,369 18-to 38-year-olds who were churched while growing up,"[6] Kevin Swanson, director of Generations with Vision conducted the Gen2 Survey, a study "exploring the correlations between different educational methods and the spiritual decisions of Millennials who were raised in the church."[7]

Swanson stated the study was "vitally important," because "it comes just as the largest numbers on historical record are migrating away from the Christian faith." He continues, "Other surveys indicate as many as 70-90% of millennials and mosaics are leaving the Christian church...this is a major spiritual collapse."[8] Swanson believes wholeheartedly that "One of the best ways to fend off the widespread secularism and apostasy of our culture is through homeschooling."[9]

The study concluded that "individuals who were home-schooled, attended church regularly, and had good relationships with their parents were most likely to remain involved in the Christian faith."[10]

APPENDIX V — RESOURCES

BOOKS:

Classical Education:

- Classical Education Made Approachable - Leigh A. Bortins
- The Core - Leigh A. Bortins
- The Question - Leigh A. Bortins
- The Conversation - Leigh A. Bortins
- The Case for Classical Education - Douglas Wilson
- The Well-Trained Mind - Jessica Wise and Susan Wise Bauer

Development:

- The Hurried Child - David Elkind
- The Way they Learn - Cynthia Ulrich Tobias
- The Strong Willed Child - Dr. James Dobson

Biblical Worldview:

- Assumptions that Affect our Lives - Christian Overman
- Love Your God with all Your Mind - J.P. Moreland
- Total Truth - Nancy Pearcy

Marriage & Family:

- The Meaning of Marriage - Timothy Keller
- Parenting Sensibly - Lynda Satre, www.parentingsensibly.com

Curriculum Reviews:

- www.thehomeschoolmom.com/homeschool-curriculum-reviews/
- www.cathyduffyreviews.com

Organizations:

- www.hslda.org
- www.hspn.net/homeschool-sports-pulse
- www.4-h.org
- www.classicalconversations.com
- www.them.company

HOMESCHOOL CHECKLIST

- Pray for guidance and strength.
- Check your state requirements for homeschooling - www.HSLDA.org - Homeschool Legal Defense

Association's website is an excellent resource. Considering joining their organization.

- Fill out a Notice of Intent to Homeschool, or similar forms with your school board if required.
- Set Goals - take some time to consider your main focus for the year. It can be for the whole family or for each child. Consider spiritual, academics, and non-academics and/or all of the above.
- Budget - set aside money for curriculum, supplies, field trips and projects.
- Methods - determine what educational model you want to use.
- Curriculum - You can use the same publisher for all subjects or mix and match. Most curriculums list the scope and sequence for their material and the skills taught. These are helpful for recording keeping and focus.
- Materials - list and purchase school supplies.
- Organization - Set up an area in your home where you will "do school." It can be as formal as a separate room with desks and a white board, or as informal as the kitchen table and storage container for books.
- Discipline - set clear expectations and consequences, understanding that in this area (and others) you may have to adjust as you gain more experience. It is important to begin with a plan, and for children to know the expectations.
- Daily Planning and Record Keeping - Again, know your state requirements. Some states, such as PA, have high regulations and others (NM) have low regulations. Decide for your home how you will plan and record your daily, weekly, and monthly schedule, including both school and non school activities.

Protect your teaching time. Whenever possible, it is helpful to schedule all outings and extras in the late afternoon or on a single day.

- Start - you will discover your own rhythm and flow.
- Evaluate - either once a month, quarter or semester, evaluate your routine and plans. Review your goals and objectives, adjust where you need to, and continue with what is working.

ENDNOTES

Preface

1. "BibleGateway." Proverbs 22:6 – *NKJV- Bible Gateway.* Biblegateway.com. n.d. Web. 15 Jan. 2016.

2. BibleGateway." *Ephesians 6:4 – NKJV.*

3. BibleGateway." *Deuteronomy 11:19-21 – NKJV.*

Introduction

1. "By 1993, home education was legal in all 50 states." Somerville, Scott W., Esq. "HSLDAThe Politics of Survival: Home Schoolers and the Law." *HSLDA The Politics of Survival: Home schoolers and the Law. HSLDA,* 2016. Web. 29 Sept. 2016.

Chapter 1

1. "Socialization" — *Dictionary.com unabridged.* Random House, Inc. 30 Jan. 2017.

2. Giddens, Anthony, Mitchell Duneier, Richard P. Apple-baum, and Deborah Carr. *Essentials of Sociology.* 3rd ed. (New York: W.W. NORTONS & COMPANY, 2011), p. 40.

Chapter 2

1. "Socialization, Basic Concepts of Sociology Guide." *Socialization, Basic Concepts of Sociology Guide.* 2016 Sociology Guide.Com, 2016. Web. 04 July 2017.

2. Konnikova, Maria. "The Limits of Friendship." The New Yorker. The New Yorker, 08 Oct. 2014. Web. 27 Apr. 2017.

3. Sizer, Bridget Bentz. "Socialization: Trackling Home-schooling's "S" Work." PBS. Public Broadcasting Service, 31 Oct. 2011. Web. 03 May 2017.

4. *Ibid.*

5. Haverluck, Michael F. "Socialization: Homeschooling vs. Schools." Socialization: Homeschooling Schools-US-CBN News- Christian News 24-7-CBN News, 2 May 2007. Web. 03 May 2017.

6. Sizer, Bridget Bentz. "Socialization: Trackling Home-schooling's "S" Work." PBS. Public Broadcasting Service, 31 Oct. 2011. Web. 03 May 2017.

7. Zacharias, Ravi K. *Jesus Among Other Gods: The Absolute Claims of the Christian Message.* Nashville TN: Work Pub., 2000. Print.6.

8. Haverluck, Michael F. "Socialization: Homeschooling VS Schools." Socialization: Homeschooling Schools-US-CBN News- Christian News 24-7-CBN News, 2 May 2007. Web. 03 May 2017.

9. *Ibid.*

10. "About NEA." *NEA.*National Education Association, 2015. Web. 03 May 2017.

Chapter 3

Aristotle and C.K. Chesterton

1. Moreland, J. P. *Love Your God with All Your Mind: The Role of Reason in the Life of the Soul*. Colorado Springs, CO: NavPress, 1997. Print. 57.

2. "At These 10 Universities, Freshmen Are Most Likely to Return. *"Freshman Retention Rate at National Universities*. U.S. News and World Report LP, 2016. Web.30 Sept. 2016

3. Urban, Tim. "Why Generation Y Yuppies Are Unhappy." *Wait but Why*. Wait but Why, 2016. Web. 13 July 2016

4. Hicks, David V. Norms & Nobility: *A Treatise on Education*. Lanham, MD: U of America, 1999. Print. 22.

5. *Ibid.*

6. Luther-King, Dr. Martin, "The Purpose of Education."*Dr.MartinLutherKingJr.com* – *The Purpose Of Education*. Humane.net,n.d. *Web*, 20 July 2017

7. Bertrand Russell quoted in Kantanbutra, Burin. "To Improve Education We Must Revise Objectives." *The National*. Thenationalmultimedia.com, 14 Dec. 2014. Web. 15 May 2016.

8. "Judge" Merriam-Webster. Merriam-Webster, 2017. Web. 25 Sept. 2017.

9. Moreland, J.P. *Love Your God With All Your Mind, p. 3.*

Chapter 5

1. Ray, Brian D., Ph. D. "National Home Education Research Institute." *Research Facts on Homeschooling | Research*. National Home Educational Research Institute, 23 Mar. 2016. Web. 17 Feb. 2017.

2. Maxwell, J.C. *15 Invaluable Laws of Growth: Live Them and Reach Your Potential*. New York: Center Street, 2014, p. 6.

3. *Ibid.*

Chapter 6

1. Toppo, Greg. "Respect at School in Decline, Survey Shows." *USA Today.* Gannett Satellite Information Network, 23 Jan. 2014.Web. 18. Feb. 2017.

Chapter 7

1. Ray, Brian D., Ph. D. "National Home Education Research Institute." *Research Facts on Homeschooling | Research.* National Home Educational Research Institute, 23 Mar. 2016. Web. 17 Feb. 2017.

2. *Ibid.*

Chapter 8

Maxwell, J.C. *15 Invaluable Laws of Growth: Live Them and Reach Your Potential.* New York: Center Street, 2014. Print. Chapter 1 – the Law of Intentionality – Growth Just doesn't happen.

1. *Ibid., p. 2.*

2. *Ibid., p. 3.*

3. *Ibid ., p. 5.*

4. Ament, Phil. " Fascinating Facts about the Invention of Post-it Notes by Arther Fry and Spencer Silver in 1974." *Post-it Note History—Invention of Post-it Notes.* The Great Idea Finder, 30 May 2006. Web. 09 Nov. 2016.

5. *Ibid.*

6. Maxwell, John, *15 Invaluable Laws of Growth: Live Them and Reach Your Potential.*

7. *Ibid., p. 6.*

8. "A Quote from Philosophical Dictionary." *Quote by C.S. Lewis: "Aim at Heaven and You Will Get Earth Thrown*

In..."Goodreads Inc., 2016. *Web.* 12 *Sept.* 2016.

9. "A Quote from The Joyful Christina." *Quote by Voltaire: "Le Mieux Est Liennemi Du Bien. The Perfect Is..."Goodreads Inc.,* 2016. *Web.* 19 *Jan.* 2017.

10. Maxwell, John, 15 *Invaluable Laws of Growth: Live Them and Reach Your Potential., p.* 8.

11. Ibid., p. 9.

12. *A League of Their Own.* Dir. Penny Marshall. Perf. Gena Davis, Tom Hanks. MLB Networks, 1993. DVD.

13. Maxwell, John, 15 *Invaluable Laws of Growth: Live Them and Reach Your Potential.*

14. Story is summarized from Day Two Vignette for Classical Conversations Practicum, 2015.

Chapter 10

1. "Appendix B." *Classical Education Made Approachable.* West End: Classical Conversations MultiMedia, 2011, p. 76-77.

2. Laura Vanderkam. "Their school day and your work day do not have to mirror each other exactly," says Pamela Price, author of *How to Work and Home school.*

3. Pendersen, James M. Summer verses School" *Google Books. Rowan & Littlefield, n.d.* Web. 21 July 2016.

Chapter 12

1. "History of Preschool in the United States." *Chris Glavin.* K12academics.com, 2016. Web. 16 Mar. 2016.

2. Lewis Brown, Laura. "Comparing Preschool Philosophies: Play-Based vs. Academic." PBS, 2016. Web 16 Sept 2016.

3. "Appendix B." *Classical Education Made Approachable.* West End: Classical Conversations MultiMedia, 2011. Print.

4. Englebright Fox, Jill, Ph. D. *Early Childhood News.* Excellence Learning Corporation 2008. Web. 16 Sept. 2016.

5. Swartz, Mallary I. "Playdough: What's Standard." Young Children (March 2005): n.d. March 2005. Web. 17 Sept 2016.

6. Vonderohe, Ruth. "The Importance of Play in Early Childhood Development Sparentsavvy." *ParenSavvy.* n.p., 2016. Web. 17 Sept 2016.

7. Moore, Heidi. "Why Play Is the Work of Childhood." *Fred Rogers Center for Early Learning & Children's Media.* Fred Rogers Center, 23 July 2015. Web. 21 Sept 2016.

8. Growth and Development, Ages 6 to 10 Years–Topic Overview." *WebMD,* WebMD 2016. Web. 17 Sept. 2016.

9. "K-8 (5-12 Years)." *Northshore University Health Services.* N.p., 2016. Web. 16 Sept 2016.

10. Miller, Christine. "On the Trivium." *Classical Christina Homeshooling: On the Trivium.* Classical Christian Homeschooling: Classical Education at Home, 2003. Web 13 Apr. 2016 Web 15 Sept 2016.

11. Jorgensen, Dr. "Why Aren't My Child's Baby Teeth Falling Out?" The Jorgensen Orthodontics Blog. Jorgensen Orthodontics, 20 Oct. 2011. Web. 18 June 2016.

12. "Losing Baby Teeth: What to Expect and When | BabyCenter." *BabyCenter.* BabyCenter L.L.C., 2016. Web. 14 Mar. 2016.

13. Suggate, Dr. "Late Readers Close Learning Gap. "*Science Alert.* University of Otago, 21 Dec. 2009. Web. 5 June 2016.

14. *Ibid.*

15. Classical Conversations Practicum 2016 Vignette— Jennifer Courtney testimony. Used by permission.

16. Fraga, Jili. "Being Mom To A Middle Schooler Can Be The Toughest Gig Of All." *NPR.* NPR, 29 Dec 2016. Web. 3. Jan 2017.

Chapter 13

1. Lythcott-Haims, Julie. *How to Raise an Adult: Break Free of the Overparenting Trap and Prepare Your Kid for Success.* St. Martin's Griffin, 2016.

2. Elisha. "What a Stanford Dean Says Parents Are Doing That's Ruining Their Kids" *Daily Crackle,* Dailycrackle, 23 Dec. 2016. Web. 14 Jan. 2017.

3. Ibid.

4. Covey, Stephen R. *Living the 7 Habits: Stories of Courage and Inspiration.* Simon & Schuster, 1999. p. 20.

5. Elisha. "What a Stanford Dean Says Parents Are Doing That's Ruining Their Kids."

6. Keller, Timothy, and Kathy Keller. *The Meaning of Maririage: Facing the Complexities of Commitment with the Wisdom of God.* London: Hodder &Stoughton, 2013, p. 115-116.

Appendix I

1. "Pluralistic" — *Dictionary.com unabridged.* Random House, Inc. 11 Feb. 2017.

2. Wilson, Douglas. Recovering the Lost Tools of Learning: An Approach to Distinctively Christian Education. Wheaton, IL: Crossway, 1991, p. 54.

3. "Losing Our Religion: The Growth Of the 'Nones'" NPR. NPR, 13 June 2013. Web. 30 Sept. 2016. *Greg Smith, a senior research at Pew.

Appendix II

1. Amos, Gary T., William Alber Dembski, and Richard K.

Gardiner. Never before in History: America's Inspired Birth. Dallas, TX: Foundation for Thoughts and Ethics, 2004, p 73.

2. Adam, Jordan. "Horace Mann's Impact on Education." *Study.com*. Study.com,2016. Web. 08 Oct 2016.

3. Ibid.

4. Ibid.

5. Boyd, Natalie. "The Freedmen's Bureau's Impact on Education." *Study.com*. Study.com, 2016. Web. 08 Oct. 2016.

6. Ibid.

7. Gamble, Foster. "The Origin Of Education and Mandatory Schooling." Collective Evolution. Collective Evolution. 07 Aug 2014. Web 22 Oct 2016.

8. Walia Arjun. "The Origin of Education and Mandatory Schooling." Collective Evolution, 7 Aug. 2014. Web. 12 October 2016.

9. Bidwell, Allie. "The History of Common Core State Standards." U.S. News &World Report. U.S. News & World Report, 7 Feb. 2014. Web. 08 Sept 2016.

10. Amos, Gary T., William Alber Dembski, and Richard K. Gardiner. Never before in History, p. 16.

11. "AdolfHitler Quotes. BrainyQuote. Xplore, 2016. Wec. 25 July 2016.

12. "AbrahamLincoln Quotes. BrainyQuote. Xplore, 2016. Wec. 25 July 2016.

13. "JosephStalin Quotes. BrainyQuote. Xplore, 2016. Wec. 25 July 2016.

14. "Wilson, Douglas. *The Case for Classical Christian Education*. Wheaton, ILL: Crossway, 2003, p. 26.

Appendix III

1. "US Supreme Court Decisions. "The Secular Web. Secular Coalition of America, 2016. Web. 8 July 2016."

Appendix IV

1. Hornyak, Lynne. "Summary of the Minutes: Mid-Winter Executive Committee Meeting. *"PsycEXTRA Dataset* (2016): n.pag. *PDF.* Web:
https://ra.nea.org/wp-content/uploads/2017/05/Resolutions_Summary_of_Winter_Committee_Meeting_Actions_2017-1.pdf

2. "Common Core Math Strives towards Goal of "Social Justice." *HSLDA* 2014. Web 9 Sept. 2015.

3. McLeod, Soul, "Saul McLeod." Simply Psychology, Creative Commons, 2008. Web. 07 Sept. 2016.

4. Gilbert K Chesterton Quotes." *Brainy Quote,* Xplore, 2017, Web. 05 Sept. 2016.

5. Lipka, Michael. "Why America's 'Nones' Left Religion Behind." *Pew Research Center*, Pew Research Center, 24 Aug. 2016.

6. Haley, Garrett. "Study Finds Homeschoolers Less Likely to Leave Faith Than Public, Private Schooled Students." *Christian News Network*, Christian News Network, 22 Feb. 2015. Web. 05 Dec. 2017.

7. Ibid.
8. Ibid.
9. Ibid.
10. Ibid.

ABOUT THE AUTHOR

Erin Barry has been home educating her children for 20 years and, with transparency, personal stories, and humor delights in each opportunity to share her experiences with other interested in any aspect of the homeschooling journey. She holds a Bachelor's degree in Education and a Masters in Clinical Christian Counseling and has taught professionally from pre-K to college.

Erin's passion is to see parents become both encouraged and empowered in their faith in Christ and fully equipped to train and guide their children toward the unique individuals they were created to be. As a veteran with Classical Conversations, an international homeschooling organization, she is grateful to Leigh Bortins and the CC programs for their dedication to providing parents with both the knowledge and tools to make home education not only possible but extremely effective and fulfilling. Within CC, Erin has been a Challenge A, B, II, III and IV Director, Tutor Trainer, Practicum Speaker and Practicum Speaker Trainer, and lead the Practicum Alumni Support Team (PAST) initiative.

Additionally, Erin and her husband, Brett, an award-winning singer/songwriter, are founders of Inseparable Lives at inseparablelives.com, a ministry devoted to nurturing Christ-centered hearts and minds who produce strong marriages, families and communities, and The Home Educated Mind at THEM.-

company, a Christ-centered community of home educators dedicated to raising up tomorrow's leaders, today.

Erin is the author of *Yes! You Can Homeschool! The Terrified Parent's Companion To Homeschool Success*. She and Brett reside in Frederick, Maryland and have successfully graduated their three children. Currently, two are in college honors programs and one is an honors college graduate.

For more information visit:

www.inseparablelives.com